# Listening To The Spirit Within

## 50 PERSPECTIVES ON FAITH

### Roland S. Martin

ROMAR Media Group
www.rolandsmartin.com

# Advanced Praise for
# *Listening to the Spirit Within*

"Behind Roland Martin's journalistic passion for examining political and cultural news, is an even deeper passion for the Word of God. *Listening to the Spirit Within* is a heartfelt message about the power of following God's voice."

*Valorie Burton, life coach and professional speaker; author of* Listen to Your Life *and* What's Really Holding You Back?

"Get ready to have your spirit lifted and fed. *Listening to the Spirit Within* is a blueprint for living a life that puts God first. In this life-changing, inspired collection of lessons backed up with scripture, Roland teaches us to use everything we say and do to the glory of God. This book is a feast for the soul and as you partake, you will be blessed."

*Terrie M. Williams, inspirational author and founder of The Stay Strong Foundation*

"*Roland Martin* is an exceptionally gifted journalist. He writes with wit and humor without blurring the lines of truth. His ability to see beyond the obvious is making him a favorite author to the learned and unlearned. The characteristic that best describes the writing of Roland is objective reality."

*Dr. Ralph Douglas West, pastor/founder, Brookhollow Baptist Church/The Church Without Walls, Houston, Texas*

"Roland's political commentaries are known to be direct and uncompromising, and he maintains that same style when it comes to his essays in *Listening to the Spirit Within*. Unwilling to try and have it both ways when it comes to his Christian walk, Roland isn't scared to challenge people of faith to hear

God's words and follow His commands. He is also honest enough to not just preach, but own up to his own failings in his walk with God."

*Cathy Hughes, founder/chairwoman, Radio One*

"*Listening to the Spirit Within* speaks to a generation today that has more wealth and knowledge than any other time in history, but often struggle with recognizing God's many blessings. An insightful guide, Roland Martin offers 50 perspectives on faith in one book that is a must-read!"

*Rev, James T. Meeks, senior pastor, Salem Baptist Church of Chicago; Illinois state senator*

"Let the spirit move you to pick up this book and read it now. Roland Martin goes deep to the heart in an inspiring book about real success at home, at work, and in the kingdom to come."

*Juan Williams*, author, *The Phony Leaders, Dead-End Movements, and Culture of Failure That Are Undermining Black America — and What We Can Do About It*

"*Listening to the Spirit Within: 50 Perspectives on Faith* is both inspirational and informative. Definitely an asset to have in our personal library."

*Darius Brooks, Grammy Award-winning gospel singer/songwriter/producer*

"*Roland Martin* offers us a clear-eyed series of essays about the importance of understanding and integrating spirituality into our everyday lives. *Listening to the Spirit Within* is a terrific book from an author trying to help us listen more to that inner voice that is always calling for the best in us."

*Gregory L. Moore, editor, The Denver Post*

"In these times common sense is not common. It takes a reaching inside to reinforce humanity against programmed society and culture. Roland Martin's latest book is a roadmap in some damn sure cloudy times. I've always dug his sharp insight, and this book is a guide we can keep close to us recognizing the God in us and not just join a shelf of other reads afterwards. Roland Martin is indeed a millennium visionary as well as a beacon clearing our spiritual vision through these modern day whippings of mass distraction, whether cultural, social or religious."

*Chuck D, founder, Public Enemy*

"Finding a spiritual peacefulness isn't easy, but this book, filled with Roland's humor and wisdom will make that inward search a lot easier."

*Michelle Singletary, nationally syndicated personal finance columnist,*
*The Washington Post; host of TV One Cable Network's "Singletary Says"*

"If you're on the doorstep of your faith, struggling, in doubt or in pain, *Listening to the Spirit Within* will offer keys to the blessings God has for you. Roland Martin's wonderful spiritual guide demystifies the scriptures and makes them relevant to the challenges of our daily lives. You'll read this gift more than once."

*Roy Johnson, editor-in-chief, Men's Fitness*

"Roland Martin is a fresh and powerful voice on the scene. His insights on life, religion, culture and politics are rich. Don't miss him!"

*Dr. Cornel West, Professor of Religion, Princeton University*

"*Listening to The Spirit Within* brings the relevance of two thousand year old wisdom to a world changing at lightning speed. It is the perfect guide for those seeking to navigate the daily demands of family, work, faith and finances from a biblical perspective. In his trademark supportive, yet 'in your face' style, Roland Martin disarms the challenges and fears that paralyze us with indecision and discouragement. I will turn to this inspiring work time and time again for fresh hope and new perspectives!"

*Encouragement Coach Felicia T. Scott, professional life coach and author of* Thrive! 7 Strategies For Extraordinary Living

"Roland Martin is that rare writer, out-of-the-box thinker, and social and political philosopher in early 21st century America: brutally honest and passionate, with the intellect to back up his musings on a range of popular and unpopular topics. Whether you agree with his assessments or not doesn't matter. What matters is that he forces you to consider America, and the world, from his vantage point. And critical perspectives like Martin's are especially important when so many are so afraid to speak their minds these days."

*Kevin Powell, author,* Someday We'll All Be Free

"Roland S. Martin delivers journalism a blunt challenge; secular and religion are not in competition; a much needed reminder."

*Lee H. Walker, President/CEO, The New Coalition for Economic and Social Change*

For more information, contact ROMAR Media Group at
P.O. Box 763127, Dallas, Texas, 75376; www.rolandsmartin.com or email to roland@rolandsmartin.com.

Unless otherwise noted, Scripture quotations marked NIV are from the Holy Bible, New International Version. Copyright 1973, 1978, 1984, International Bible Society; as well as Eugene Peterson's The Message.

Martin, Roland S.
Listening to the Spirit Within: 50 Perspectives on Faith
Roland S. Martin — 1st Edition
Published by ROMAR Media Group
ISBN: 0-9719107-2-3

Cover design by Zina Martin and Kenon White. Inside pages and back cover designed by Kenon White, www.viziondesign.com

Cover photo by Jesse Hornbuckle, www.hornbucklephoto.com
Copy editor: Keisha Chavers

# DEDICATION

*To my wife, the Rev. Jacquie Hood Martin, for being a strong woman of God who refuses to compromise the Word of the Lord. She is the embodiment of what the Scripture calls a "help mate."*

# Listening To The Spirit Within

## 50 PERSPECTIVES ON FAITH

## Roland S. Martin

## Table of Contents

# Introduction

Shhh. Did you hear that? It might have been a loud, dramatic noise or a whisper. Regardless of how loud or soft it was, the intent was clear: God is trying to speak to you and get your attention.

After reading some of the faith-based columns that I've written over the years, many people often ask me, "How did you know that it was God speaking to you?" My answer is the same as Jesus' answer in the parable in John 10:3-5: "*The watchmen opens the gate for him, and the sheep listen to his voice. He calls His own sheep by name and leads them out.*"

There is an incredible revelation in that scripture, and it relates to being attentive when God is trying to speak to us.

First, **the "watchmen" represents God.** Whether we are asleep, driving around town or at work, God is watching over us. As His sheep, we are under the care and protection of the watchmen. Why? Because when the sheep were being led, they encountered many difficult issues along the route. Some paths were rocky, and they had to brave the elements while forever being stalked by the evil wolves. We, too, are under the same duress. This journey called life requires us to listen to the voice of the watchmen — God — so that we won't be led astray. We face many difficulties in this life and the road will not always be straight and smooth. That's when the experience of the watchmen takes over so that we can be kept safe from venturing into the clutches of evil — Satan. As long as the sheep obey the watchmen, all will be well.

"**The watchmen opens the gate for him.**" We cannot execute, much less receive a vision from God, if we don't first open our minds to receive His word. How would we know what path to take if God has not told us where to go and where to begin? The sheep could crash into the gate, but all that would do is create chaos. Instead, when the shepherd opens the gates, an orderly process can occur and all the sheep will be safe. We must be patient and allow God to speak His word into our lives, and then allow God to provide the blueprint for how we are to proceed. If not, we risk rushing head first into something without a proper plan, which is a definite recipe for disaster.

**"The sheep listen to his voice."** How many times have you been that wayward sheep that is unable to hear God speak to you? The sheep must exhibit extreme obedience by listening. That is a difficult task for many of us because we often can't hear God because we are always talking or we have our minds cluttered with unnecessary thoughts. When the shepherd is speaking a vision into our lives, we must be attentive to all of it.

**"He calls his own sheep by name and leads them out."** There are billions of people in this world, but God knows you personally. Don't think you are just a number or a "back bencher" who can easily slip in and out. No! In John 21:5-11, Jesus speaks to the disciples while they are fishing. By this time Jesus had been resurrected and they couldn't see him when he asked, *"Friends, haven't you any fish?"* They didn't know who he was, but upon hearing his voice, John, the disciple whom Jesus loved, told Peter, *"It is the Lord."* John may not have been able to recognize that it was Jesus, but because of his close relationship, he knew what Jesus sounded like. Understand, the shepherd is aware of all his sheep, where they are, which one is hurt, as well as all the weaknesses and strengths. When God is ready to reveal His vision for your life, don't fret. Your name will be called and no one else will hear!

One day a man asked me why I freely discuss the vision God has given me for my life. I told him that it doesn't matter if someone else hears it because when this vision was given it had my name on it; He called my name!

A few years ago, I was at a crossroad in my life. I didn't have a full-time job and was unsure of what was next. Many folks were assuming that I was a minister and some thought that I should go into the ministry. But one day while sitting in my then-fiancée's apartment, God settled this dilemma.

He made it perfectly clear that I was to continue into the area of communications and media.

"Roland, have you ever wondered why your focus has always been on learning all aspects of media? See, I knew where you would be in 1999. I knew that no one was going to be just doing one form of media. The landscape has changed and you are in a prime position to do television, radio, newspaper and the Internet. Roland, I need you doing exactly what you are doing. I need an individual who isn't afraid to speak the truth, regardless of what others may feel. When you are doing radio, you may be speaking to more people in five minutes than some ministers will speak to in a year."

It was during this conversation that God continued to push me to keep doing what I was doing because I was in a position to address a variety of social issues through a faith-based prism. Even when I was doing a sports show on WOL-AM, we often discussed how faith and sports intersected. We discussed issues like drug abuse, domestic violence, anger management and steroid abuse.

These are issues that both Christians and non-Christians are facing in their lives, yet the platform was a sports show! Had I not made the point of listening to God, I may have gone down a path that wasn't in His will.

**"He goes on ahead of them."** Receiving a vision from God can be fulfilling, scary, daunting and challenging, all at the same time. Why? Because the vision can be so large, complex, powerful and awesome, we can't fathom getting it done. But as this scripture reveals, God will go before us. We don't have to worry about being led down the wrong path because His *"sheep follow because they know his voice."* We cannot follow a stranger who gives us troubling, unclear and conflicting information. And if we get some information that is supposedly a "word" from God, then we are told by scripture to take it to scripture to make sure it is of God (take some time and do a Bible study on false prophets and teachers). By having a true relationship with Christ, we will be able to discern what is of God and what isn't, whether at church, at work or in our homes. If it seems like a "stranger's voice," then it is a stranger's voice. Stop listening, turn away, wait to hear God's voice to confirm what is and isn't from Him.

In order for us to be in a position to hear God's voice, we must partake in a regular rotation of prayer, meditation and Bible study. I don't care how good your pastor can preach the word and how holy your mom and dad are. Every believer must engage in regular and consistent Bible study. Scripture is called "the living word" because God speaks to us and meets us at our place of need.

# Introduction

We can't listen to the spirit of God that is within us unless we make sure we have found a quiet place to hear God speak to us. In John 3:8, Jesus says, "The wind blows wherever it pleases. You hear its sound, but you cannot tell where it comes from or where it is going." So it is with everyone born of the Spirit."

When God wants to speak to us, His words are just like the wind, and we often don't hear it. Even though God can drop in on our spirit at any time, we must follow the example of Jesus, who often left the boisterous crowds and the disciples to commune with God.

As you move forward reading this book, decide the weak points in your Christian walk and commit to shoring up that area. If you have not gotten comfortable with reading and understanding scripture, get a good study Bible (I use *The Quest*; another is the New International Version Disciple's Study Bible). Again, take the time to be diligent in improving these areas of your faith. I promise that you will be enriched.

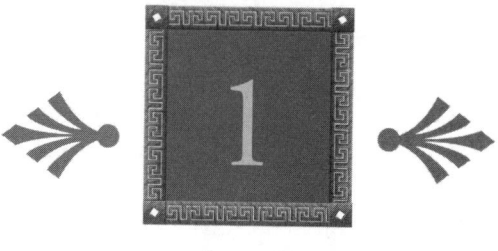

# A lesson
# in compassion
# passion

*Text focus: Jonah 4:1-4*

\*\*\*

L
ike it or not, we live in an extremely cynical world. Turn on talk radio,
a television news shows or even a movie, and folks think the world
has gone to hell with tons of people walking around with their heads
screwed on backwards. It would make even a sensible person conclude that
everyone is the ultimate sinner.

Such a pervasive view extends to the church where leaders call those who
are homosexual, adulterers and involved in crime hateful sinners who are
destroying the world. While we are called on by scripture to love one another,
we consistently throw barbs at others without extending them a helping hand
out of their situation.

The Lord made that so clear to me after reading the book of Jonah.

Jonah was one of those prophets who God blessed with the anointing, but
allowed far too much of his flesh to rule his thinking. When he was told to
go to Nineveh, Jonah took off like a babbling fool afraid of the message God
gave him. Instead of being obedient to the Word from on high, he chose to
try to hide from God, thinking that he would be forgotten.

But Jonah was greatly mistaken. Not only did God track him down, he
even caused a great storm which forced Jonah to be thrown into the sea and

swallowed by a whale. Amazing. God did all of that just to get Jonah's undivided attention. So, what has He had to do to get your attention?

When he finally went to Nineveh, Jonah told the people that they must repent for their actions or be destroyed. They did just as he instructed by fasting, changing their ways and calling on the Lord not to destroy them. But a funny thing happened. Jonah got ticked with God for showing compassion to the people of Nineveh and not sticking to his promise to destroy them. It seems that Jonah had a bit of selective memory in this regard. Just a few days earlier Jonah disobeyed a direct command from God, yet he was given a second chance. But he was angry with God for extending his compassion to those in Nineveh who followed the instructions of the anointed one.

As Jonah stormed off, huffing and puffing and pouting, he took off to watch what God would do to Nineveh. While Jonah was sitting down, the Lord allowed a vine to grow above his head to shield him from the sweltering heat. But while Jonah was sleeping, the Lord then sent a worm to eat the vine, thus depriving Jonah of the shade.

When he woke up, Jonah was hotter than all get out, and he almost passed out because of the heat. What did he do? Lament and complain that he was better off dead than alive. God then stepped in and asked Jonah why he was mad at not having shade that he had nothing to do with in the first place. In other words, he was given a gift but was upset that it no longer existed. It seems as if our dear friend Jonah had a bad case of what's-good-for-me-ain't-so-good-for-you.

And this is so true of many of us. We often complain that others shouldn't be extended grace and mercy, yet never think about all of those times we messed up, only to have God step in and place his healing hands on us. We slept with people of the opposite sex before marriage, yet we slap others upside the head for doing the same thing.

A lot of us just started tithing, but we are quick to tell our brothers and sisters they are robbing God by not giving 10 percent. Our church leaders commit sins, and we virtually strip them of their Christianity, but when we did it, we want the pastor to pray for us to be healed and made whole.

This isn't a license for us to do what we want, when we want, and not speak the truths of scripture. I will not justify sin because others say we should be tolerant and accepting of others actions. Absolutely not! My justification is tantamount to me endorsing that which I know is bad.

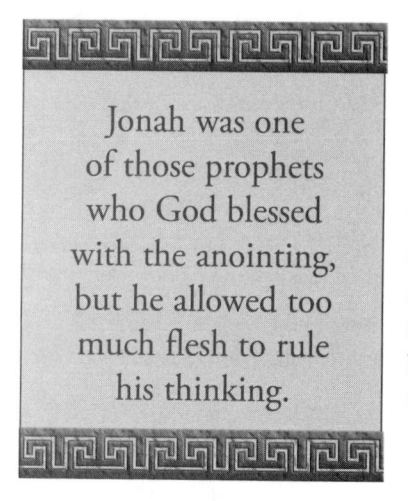

Jonah was one of those prophets who God blessed with the anointing, but he allowed too much flesh to rule his thinking.

We are supposed to hold each other accountable when we step out of line and fall short of what God has designed for us. No one should feel afraid of pulling the coattail of a friend who is married when he or she is being a little too friendly with a co-worker. If our friend, co-worker or family member is gay, we are to urge them not to engage in sex with someone of the same sex because scripture says that it is sinful. Our aim should be to encourage them to abstain from such behavior, and then to live a more Christ-like life. No one should blow off the actions of a man or woman who is verbally or physically abusive to their spouse.

We know that violence is not the key to a successful and long lasting marriage. Instead of condemning them, we are told to extend a hand of friendship and gently and use scripture to help them through their situation. When we sin we know it. The last thing we need is someone slapping us in the face. What we need to do is hold them, caress them and show them the ways of the Lord, which are clearly outlined in scripture.

I've discovered that a lot of people want to do the right thing, but they haven't the foggiest idea where to begin. We all know that it begins with accepting Jesus Christ as our Lord. And after we do that we are to follow his commands for righteous living. But when we sin, we are to completely repent, turn away from our sins and renew ourselves for God.

If we sin again, we are to follow the same steps. Proverbs says a righteous man fell seven times. We must not celebrate his sinful behavior but rejoice in the fact that he repented seven times and was willing to keep getting back up.

It takes others a little bit longer to get it right, but we are to rejoice when they finally do get it right.

The story of Jonah and Ninevah is not one where God wanted to show us the evil ways of the city and how they were obedient to his command. What jumped up in my spirit was that God used Ninevah for the purpose of teaching Jonah the need for compassion. And when he didn't get it, God had to do it again with the vine and the worm.

If you are moved in the spiritual realm to speak to someone about their wayward ways, be sure to ask God to not only put the proper words in your mouth and on your heart, but also to give you a compassionate spirit in dealing with that person by reminding you of when you were troubled and prayed for someone to shower you with compassion.

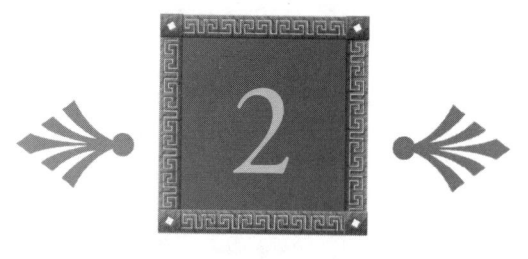

# Don't let the
# package fool you

*Text focus: 1 Samuel 8-10*

***

W hen driving to the store or even sitting on an airplane, I often look over at my wife and say to myself, "My God, this is a beautiful woman!" I can't help but love her sunny smile, fat cheeks, brown eyes and shapely figure.

She always laughs when I say it — which isn't enough — but I really do mean it with all my heart and soul. It's not the physical that I am most speaking of (although her outward appearance is one of a cutie) but her spirit. Her heart is so pure and warm that there is often a glow all around her.

People have said for years that beauty is only skin deep and it doesn't matter what's on the outside, but it is what's on the inside that counts. I concur with those statements, but I honestly believe that we judge people for their outward appearance.

We can talk all day about being the nice, loving Christian who looks past someone's hair, face and body, but nine out of 10 times it was a physical attraction that made us want to seek out our mate. That's okay, as long as we keep it all in proper perspective.

The tendency to look at outward appearances when making decisions is often the downfall of many people today. We aren't alone in this area; we're just following the footsteps of the children of Israel during biblical days.

In 1 Samuel 8, Israel demanded that the prophet Samuel appoint them a king because he was an old man and his sons were not suitable because they didn't "walk in his ways." Samuel resisted their overtures, but they continued. It seems as if the elders had fallen into the idol worship that was common among their enemies and they sought a ruler to guide them through their difficult times. This thinking was silly considering God had his hand on them from the moment they left Egypt, but like disobedient children, they were more willing to follow flesh instead of spirit.

When Samuel went looking for a king, God led him to a man who was considered the most handsome of all men in the land — Saul. Not only were good looks a requirement for leadership, he also was taller than any man, which they considered a key ingredient (1 Samuel 9:2).

After Samuel anointed Saul as king he went before the people to tell them of his choice. But a funny thing happened along the way: Saul went into hiding. That's right. Here he was about to be crowned the king of Israel after being anointed by the prophet and after the Holy Spirit had overtaken him, yet he chose to go run and hide. Even from the outset, Saul didn't have the intestinal fortitude to walk in the way of the Lord.

If we continue to read the rest of 1 Samuel and 2 Samuel, we get a pretty good idea of Sault as a leader. Although God had warned Israel that the king they so desired would turn out to be nothing but a tyrant, (1 Samuel 8:10-22) they didn't care.

The man who was so handsome and so tall turned their lives into a living hell because of his disobedience of the Lord and his envious spirit. The people of Israel had no one else to blame but themselves. They could have relented from their wishes for a king, especially when he chose to run and hide, but they didn't.

This is often the case with so many of us today. We know within our heart, mind and soul that a particular job, so-called friend, potential husband or wife or activity we want to do is not right for us, yet we continue to say, "I want it. I want it." Some even claim such headaches in the name of Jesus.

Instead of seeking God and asking, "Is this in your will?" we choose to go down our own path. And when that path leads to pain, heartache, and agony, we do just what Israel did: Turn to God and ask to be saved.

God is a God of grace and mercy, but wouldn't it be nice if we just tried to follow Him instead of trying to fulfill our fleshly desires? Samuel was the vessel God used to speak to his people, but they blew him off and decided to choose their own destiny.

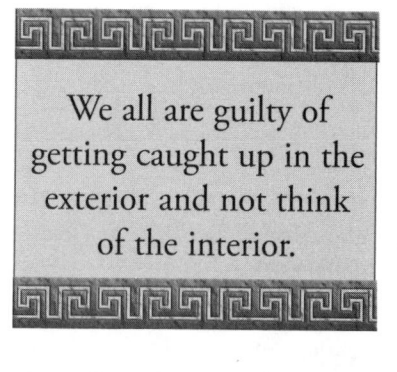

We all are guilty of getting caught up in the exterior and not think of the interior.

I would hope that each of you would choose to ignore the external of a person or situation and focus on the hidden attributes. Yes, the salary and corner office of that new job may look enticing and it may be just what you think you need, but you haven't even thought about the evil spirits that lurk in that place of employment. You might be getting a big boost in your pay, but you may end up paying the ultimate price in terms of stress, anxiety and potential illness because of what that job takes out of you.

The same goes for our relationships with friends or a potential mate. When we meet them all is well and things are going fine. But the baggage they bring to the relationship may end up weighing you down and causing you to go nuts while trying to fend off their stuff. You might look up and find that your "friend" ended up being a negative influence on your children and leading them into things that are not of God. That mate with the perfect body, nice set of teeth and wonderful bank account may be a disaster waiting to happen. Once the shades are pulled back you could very well discover a materialistic and aggressive person with low self-esteem who ends up being so high-maintenance that all you want to do is run for cover.

Let's just be honest. At one time or another we have made a decision for what we thought was right and just, but it was done with all the wrong intentions. If you are in that kind of situation you must look to the Father to lead you out of your wilderness experience and into a new beginning. And that may require some hard choices on your part. That job may be great and meet your financial needs, but the price you may be paying is your life or state of mind.

And I will tell you in a minute that there is no amount of money that could make me risk those two! We should always seek the Lord and ask Him for his guidance and divine revelation in all aspects of our life. I can tell you by experience that God will lead you out of your troubles. It may require some major adjustments on your part — houses and cars may have to be sold to downsize to a more affordable lifestyle, and eating out several times a week may cease. But the overwhelming weight of that job will be lifted, which will make a world of difference in your countenance and daily life.

Again, we all are guilty of getting caught up in the exterior and not think of the interior. But when we allow God to come into our hearts to take complete control, He will give us the freedom to think clearly and openly, and discern what is proper for us.

If that is you, just go to a quiet place and ask God to reveal His will. If it means letting something or someone go, then do it. You will definitely see a change for the good.

# Living with an anointed woman

*Text focus: Judges 4:4*
\*\*\*

We all have heard the old adage that behind every good man is a good woman and behind every good woman is a good man. That statement is no truer than when it comes to the husband of Prophetess Deborah, Lappidoth.

If you take a survey of the Bible you will find that there is no mention of Lappidoth other than in Judges 4:4. We have no understanding of his lineage, what kind of man he was and what he did for a living. But using my sanctified imagination, I would bet that Lappidoth was truly an Ephesians man who loved his wife like Christ loved the church and honored her in everything he did.

How could I make such a suggestion, you ask? That revelation came a few weeks ago while in New York. I was working with *Savoy* Magazine and I went to a Bible study that the editor-in-chief, Roy Johnson, and his wife attend. They were studying the leadership of Deborah, and as I began to read the text, the Lord began to speak in an awesome way.

Lappidoth had to be an awesome man of God because there is nowhere in Judges 4 where we read about Deborah having to fight and scrap in order to use her God-given gifts in ministry as well as do her job as a leader.

There are many men today who aren't like Lappidoth. They don't encourage, support or endorse the spiritual gifts of their wives. Instead, they work like crazy to limit their work within the church and the kingdom of God.

What these men don't understand is that they are limiting the blessings God has in store for their family by not being like Lappidoth and encouraging their wives in the task that God has given them. Deborah felt comfortable with her role of sorting out disputes in Israel, and having a solid and loving home life makes that job so much easier.

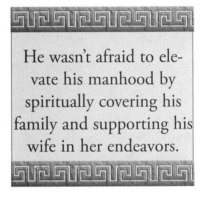

He wasn't afraid to elevate his manhood by spiritually covering his family and supporting his wife in her endeavors.

Second, Lappidoth obviously wasn't a man who tripped on his wife working. While Deborah was out working on behalf of Israel, Lappidoth could have been one of those men who wonder where the dinner is and why the kids aren't being taken care of and why the house isn't clean. He didn't complain, he didn't spend his day talking about me, me, me. I wouldn't be surprised if Lappidoth wasn't holding down the fort and praying for his wife while she was away from home leading Israel in battle.

Lastly, Lappidoth had to recognize the leadership qualities in his wife, and he wasn't afraid to elevate his manhood by spiritually covering his family and supporting his wife in her endeavors. In biblical days women just didn't lead men. But at that time Israel was sorely lacking in male leadership (70 percent of black homes today are run by single women. There are a whole lot of Deborahs in black America today) and Deborah had to step in and fill that role. Even when the prophetess told Barak that God had given them the victory at Mount Tabor, he chickened out and said he wouldn't go if she didn't come with him. Her response? *"Very well,"* she says in Judges 4:9. *"I will go with you. But because of the way you are going about this, the honor will not be yours for the Lord will hand Sisera over to a woman."*

Far too many men have used Scripture as a steel hand to suppress the leadership qualities of women. A lot of men, erroneous in my opinion, are adamant that women should not be pastors and preach the Gospel. Yet by making such a statement they are freely admitting that God is not omnipotent and omnipresent. God has the power to anoint anyone to act as a vessel to build the kingdom.

Scripture should free us from an oppressive spirit, not contribute to it. Lappidoth was the kind of man who put his ego aside and praised the Lord for his wife's leadership skills and for her strengths being recognized by the people of Israel.

If you're a man, how do you stack up against Lappidoth? If you are a woman, does your man follow in the footsteps of Lappidoth? If the answer is no to the latter or the former, then the two of you need to begin to have some serious conversations as it relates to your spiritual talents.

Deborah's first responsibility was to accept her anointing and fulfill the job God required of her. Her second role was to be a wife. And her job came third. That is the spiritual order that God has given all of us. Although I may be the head of my household, my job should never come before my spouse or my dedication to God.

In these days where men have seriously abdicated their responsibility, it is high time that more of us assume the role of Lappidoth and encourage, support, pray and cover our wives, sisters and mothers. The Lord is not only judging us by what he gives us to do, but also by the way we act and respond to the person he has put us with.

# An uncompromising word

*Text focus: Galatians 1*
***

If you go down the list of the great theologians, evangelists, prophets and preachers, one of the defining characteristics they all have is an unwavering commitment to the Word of God.

Dietrich Bonhoeffer. Martin Luther. Richard Allen. C.H. Spurgeon. Charles Mason. These were individuals who remained steadfast to the word of God and who didn't resort to histrionics in order to speak directly to the needs and desires of the people who sat under their leadership.

If only we could return to their words, but more importantly, follow in their footsteps!

Today, it seems that the word of God has been taken by Madison Avenue and refined to make it more palatable to an audience that holds numerous degrees, but is wholly ignorant of scripture.

That lack of understanding could be the result of ministers who are preaching a gospel that is incomplete, suspect and driven by ego.

Don't get me wrong. There are countless individuals who are directly addressing the desperate needs of souls who are so twisted and confused that they are on the verge of going crazy.

My criticism is with the purveyors of goodness — those who preach everyday-is-a-sunny-day gospel. Sitting under this teaching often feels like a seminar or workshop rather than church. In fact, there are a number of ministers who have chosen to call themselves motivational speakers. Instead of accepting the lofty position that God has given them, they have chosen to "motivate" the sheep rather than convict them.

> Many churches are falling into the trap and deciding not to even bring up the one word that really defines our worldly existence: sin.

But of course, don't leave out the Spiritual Platinum Club. These are the so-called spreaders of the truth who ignore most of the Bible, except for the scripture that speaks directly to tithes, offerings and money. These "prosperity worshippers" are constantly fed the name-it-and-claim-it mantra, even though it may not be in God's will for you to drive a Jaguar or Mercedes.

Maybe these are the folks Paul warned us about in Galatians 1. They seem to preach a gospel that is far different than what he was taught.

If you really sit back and study the trends, many churches are falling into the trap and deciding not to even bring up the one word that really defines our worldly existence: sin.

I suppose a lot of this can be traced back to the need to make people feel comfortable, in their cushioned suits, in today's palatial palaces of worship. God forbid the air conditioning go out! We might just have to cancel church for fear of our members sweating!

Yet the reality is we should be sweating, even if the AC is working just fine. There are countless times when I have been grateful to sit under my pastor and hear him preach on sin and what I need to do to rid it from my life. It wasn't pleasant to hear. As the Rev. Frederick D. Haynes III, senior pastor of Friendship-West Baptist Church in Dallas, is fond of saying, "I'm bowling down your alley and sitting in your pew." But sometimes we have to get a dose of reality and shock us out of the doldrums of life, even when it makes us squirm in our seat.

A few years ago I heard Bishop Eddie L. Long preach to his flock about living healthier lives.

A number of the folks at his church, New Birth Missionary Baptist Church in Atlanta, were obese. That's not shocking; studies show that the majority of Americans are overweight or obese. I'm sure Long's members didn't see their eating as being wrong, but not taking care of our temple — the body — is a Godly concept.

*"Do you not know that your body is a temple of the Holy Spirit, who is in you, whom you have received from God? You are not your own; you were bought at a price. Therefore honor God with your body."* 1 Corinthians 6:19-20 (NIV).

Long told his church that he would begin to preach on the issue to affect change in the kingdom of God.

There are other pastors who take a hard stance against domestic violence.

They are quick to speak directly to men who beat their wives and girlfriends, even if it means showing up at his job to take him out for *"a little counseling."*

The wife of a pastor in Houston told their minister of music that he would have give up his gay lifestyle or leave his post. She took seriously the scriptures that speak against homosexuality, as well as 1 Timothy 3:2: *"Here is a trustworthy saying: If anyone sets his heart on being an overseer, he desires a noble task. Now the overseer must be above reproach, the husband of but one wife, temperate, self-controlled, respectable, hospitable, able to teach, not given to drunkenness, not violent but gentle, not quarrelsome, not a lover of money."*

The minister of music is in charge of the praise and worship, which is our way of showing God our gratitude for his grace and mercy. That means that this minister is in charge of administering specifically to the needs of the church through music. If that person is living a life that is unbecoming of Christ, how can he or she effectively minister to the flock?

This particular minister of music left, but the pastor and his wife remained focused on having ministry leaders who lived according to God's purpose.

When our churches begin to stray from the teachings of Christ, it is vital that we hold them accountable. The body of Christ cannot grow effectively when we compromise the word of God in order to make people feel at ease.

Jesus told us in Matthew 5:13 that *"you are the salt of the earth. But if the salt loses its saltiness, how can it be made salty again? It is no longer good for anything, except to be thrown out and trampled by men."*

Sometimes the word of God is bitter, painful, and hard on the ears. But just like salt, it can also preserve us and condition us to be used again and again.

Our children hate to be disciplined when they do wrong, and God uses his preachers, teachers and ministers to discipline us in the ways of — the Lord.

Otherwise, we risk the possibility of going through this world as a wild child who is unwilling to live in the model of Christ.

Make the effort to be bold and tough. Don't allow the delicate sensibilities of your friends and church family to alter the word that God has placed in your spirit. It just might be the right thing they need to hear in order to save their life from the pain and degradation of eternal sin.

# Fighting the distraction

*Text focus: Romans 12:2*
***

For the last several weeks, I have been experiencing great difficulty sleeping.

I often lie in the bed for hours on end, desperately trying to get some shut—eye before I have to awake for another long day. Even now, I write this at 2:43 a.m. because of another night of constant tossing and turning.

Tired of sleepless nights, I went into meditation two weeks ago while on a cruise to ask God what in the heck was going on. With the sweet breeze coming off the calming waters of the Caribbean, I had to breakdown and say, "God, what is happening? Is there something that you are trying to tell me that I have not been getting?"

His reply was as quick and concise as my question.

"Yes," He replied. "I have asked and asked you to read, study and prepare for what I have for you to do, yet you have continued to offer excuses."

Knowing full well what He was talking about, I tried to do one of those "Yea, I know I haven't been on my job" statements. But there was little compassion. "You have said that before. As a result, I am going to require you to read three Bible chapters a night because I no longer have time for you to do this on your own schedule. There are things I need you to say, do and write and I can't afford to wait for your schedule."

For two weeks I heeded this call. But last week, fighting allergies and downing Nyquil like crazy, I didn't do that. A brother was tired and sleepy. I wanted to get some rest. But while resting on my wife's hips and falling into a comfortable sleep, I began to hear a phone ring. I tried to ignore the phone, but it kept ringing and ringing and ringing. Tired of it, I finally woke up, only to discover that the phone was only in the spirit. At that moment God said, "Get up and read those three chapters." God didn't care that I was tired and sick. "You had all day to read three chapters. I didn't tell you to read them late at night. You didn't mind reading that other book. You could have been reading one chapter at breakfast, one at lunch and the other at dinner." Recognizing the error of my ways, I got up and read those three chapters.

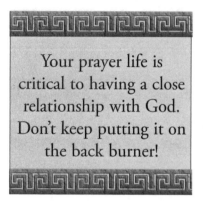

Your prayer life is critical to having a close relationship with God. Don't keep putting it on the back burner!

With all of the things I am involved in, God had to show me that my busy life was filled with so many distractions that I would often fail to do what he had required of me because I was too busy focusing on things that aren't as important. Yes, my job is vital because it pays the bills, but there is a word that will remain dormant unless I pick up my Bible and read it. The organizations I belong to are doing some good things, yet if I don't consistently study the Word, how will I be able to assist a soul who I come across?

The distractions in our life can come in many forms: TV, radio, books, food, friends, family, the phone, cleaning, cooking, and the list goes and on. A distraction is essentially anything that removes our mind, body and spirit away from something that we know is much more important. I'm an avid consumer of information and I can easily spend three to four hours on the Internet, reading and studying all kinds of Web sites. I also have more than 500 books at home and I am always reading. But I've had to learn to fight the distractions around me and force myself to sit down, go into my prayer room, pick up my Bible and begin to read and study.

Growing spiritually is always a major New Year's resolution. The easiest way to break that resolution is falling into the trap of putting God last on your priority list. I know the task may seem daunting but it really isn't. Each and every single one of us has 24 hours in a day to work with. The question of the day is: How will we make God a priority in that time?

**Here are some suggestions:**

1. **Commit to a daily prayer routine.** Maybe it's 10 to 30 minutes when you wake up or go to sleep. It doesn't matter when, just set your mind to it and make it happen.

2. **Use technology to your benefit.** Are you always on the go and can't grab your Bible and read it? No problem. Get the Bible on tape or CD and listen to it on your way to work. Study can be done with your eyes or ears. Set your Palm Pilot or Microsoft Outlook to beep daily with the reminder, "Read your Bible!" or "PRAY!" The alarm will go off daily and it will keep you on schedule. If it works with your work schedule, why can't it be a wonderful way to get your spiritual life right?!

3. **Get a prayer or accountability partner.** If a spotter is good when it comes to working out at the gym, get someone who can do the same for your prayer life. When I was single, I had a friend who I would call (or she would call me) daily and we would read a Bible verse and then pray. That person is accountable to you and you are accountable to them. Remember: You want someone who isn't lazy and won't blow you off.

4. **Take your time reading the Bible.** How many people have wanted to read the Bible by starting at Genesis? But by June, they have barely gotten to Numbers. And by the end of the

year, they are still stuck in Psalms. Don't try to read the Bible in one week. Focus on one chapter at a time or go to a Christian bookstore and get a good Bible study guide or visit BibleGateway.com.

Your prayer life is critical to having a close relationship with God. Don't keep putting it on the back burner!

# Looking for a few
# Godly men: Fear Him

*Text focus: 2 Samuel 23*
***

A few weeks ago the men of my church in Houston were asked to stand by our associate pastor. The men's retreat was coming up and they had to keep extending the registration because not enough men had registered. Upon telling the congregation that the church had more than 3,000 men on the rolls yet less than 300 applied for the conference, an old tactic was used: compare the number of men attending their conference to the number of women attending their conference.

Such a comparison is always a waste of time because in most cases, women in the church have always outnumbered the men when it came to attending such functions. Men have been given the role as head of household by God, yet for some reason they continuously refuse to participate in programs that can assist them in developing as better men of God, husbands, fathers, workers and leaders.

I used to belong to the group that would make such comparisons, but after reading about David's Mighty Men in 2 Samuel, the Lord changed my mind and showed me a new way of thinking.

When you take a stroll through 2 Samuel 23 you will discover that David commanded a mighty battalion of men who were the fiercest of all warriors in Israel. They were highly skilled fighters, and they men were loyal to David as their leader and would do anything to protect him. In addition, they all had the most important characteristics of strong men of God: their egos were in check, and they were disciplined, committed and focused. This posture was necessary because had they possessed major attitudes and refused to follow orders, their lives would be at risk as well as the future of Israel.

> We need to turn our attention to small bands of men who are committed to being Godly men and to go deep into scripture in order to learn how to lead God's way.

Modern day men can learn a lot from David's Mighty Men because similar efforts should be undertaken in churches and ministries across the country. We shouldn't place all of our focus on having male conferences with thousands of men in attendance if they are not fully focused on learning what is required to be Godly men and men of honor. In other words, there is no need to take up space with dead weight.

I can recall attending a church sponsored men's retreat two years ago that left me angry and bitter. After a day of recreation, we had dinner and then a church service. Yet after the 1 ½ hour service, the tables came out so the men could play cards, dominoes, eat sandwiches and do more fellowship. My anger boiled over because there were men in the room who came there with major problems, yet they were leaving the same way they came: broken.

When it comes to men, we treat them with kid gloves and give in to athletics, the big screen televisions and all of the manly things we think guys do when they get together. We are often afraid to challenge them spiritually and get them into major conversations about their troubles and difficulties as husbands and fathers. We are afraid to tell them how to be strong men in the workplace. But what God showed me after that weekend was not to focus on numbers. Instead, go after a small battalion.

We need to turn our attention to small bands of men who are committed to being Godly men and to go deep into scripture in order to learn how to lead God's way. David wasn't worried about having every man at his side to fight. He only wanted highly skilled men who would never give up when in battle.

Let's follow David's lead and seek small groups of men who are committed to being strong Christians. These accountability groups should be there for one another in addition to reading, studying and delving deep into scripture. And once trained, they can represent Christ through their actions. Everything about these men should say God: the way they walk, talk and act. Once these men are a strong fighting unit, they will then use their skills at spiritual warfare to go out and capture other men, take them under their wings and teach them how to be stronger men of God.

Satan knows that the destruction of the family largely starts with the man.

By the Lord giving man authority and dominion over everything on Earth (Genesis 1:28), Satan and all evil spirits know that if the man is taken down it is easier to run amok in the lives of women and children. That's why it's important for us to have strong men who are unafraid to represent God and to lead their families properly. It must be understood that when a family is destroyed, a church is destroyed as well. And when a church is destroyed, the community is destroyed. When a community is leveled, a city is rendered useless. When the city is no longer operational the state can't function properly. And destroyed states mean a dysfunctional nation.

Godly men, our brothers are out of order. Our men are bedding women and leaving them to raise kids without a loving and nurturing father figure. Others have to endure being the mother and father for countless children, many of who don't even know who their father is. Those same kids grow up to be problem children who get involved in drugs, alcohol and commit crimes. If they don't, many grow up to repeat the same sins as the fathers they never knew.

This cycle of destruction must end. But in order for it to do so it must begin with men of honor assuming their place and becoming committed and convicted in the Holy Spirit. Our aim is not to wait until every man is on board. All we need is a few good men to form a mighty battalion and then we're on our way.

If you're one of those men who desire to change your life, make the commitment right now to get involved in your men's ministry. Start going to Bible study and bring your sons and daughters along. Don't rely on your wife's prayers, you begin to lead the prayers at lunch or dinner and begin to be a strong man in the Word. If you don't know where to start or are afraid, drop me an e-mail and I can provide you with some advice and tools to get you started on the right road.

The definition of authentic manhood is not Barry Bonds, Kurt Warner or some other athlete or high-powered executive. It's those men named Benaiah, Abishai, Eleazar and the others who stood side-by-side with David to fight for their country.

Gentleman, now it's time to fight to protect our borders. We must walk in divine order. This is a call to arms. It's time to man up.

# Looking for a few Godly men: A mighty battalion

*Text focus: Psalms 111:10, Psalms 112:1-2*

***

L et me be the first to say that I have never been buddy-buddy with my dad. In fact, I have always been downright fearful of the man. Although some of you are wincing right now, it must be understood that I love my dad immensely. But he has never made the effort to try to be my best friend. As he has said before, it's not his job to be my best friend but my father.

Many of us have this issue confused. We live in a day and time when mothers and fathers are desperately trying to "relate" to their children by being their friends. While this is a noble idea, all that does is reduce the authority of the parent and seriously limit their effectiveness in raising and steering that child in the proper direction.

As I read today's scripture focus in Psalms, I was initially shocked to read such language: "*The fear of the Lord is the beginning of wisdom; all who follow his precepts have good understanding.*" I quickly thought, "*Man, what kind of God would issue such stern language that we should fear him?*" My worldly mind says he should be a loving father who cares for us, picks us up when we are down, caresses and comforts us when we are hurt and walks us through the difficult times of life. But the Lord quickly reminded me that a loving father does all of those things, yet we are to fear our heavenly father because he has laid down the law and we are to follow his every command. In Psalms 112 it says, *"Blessed is the man who fears the Lord, who finds great delight in his commands."*

Read that verse again. *"Blessed is the man who fears the Lord, who finds great delight in his commands."* First of all, the sentence begins with the word blessed. In effect it says that we begin blessed when we fear the Lord. That is because when we operate in His will, God loves us and looks after us. He instructs us to fear Him and by doing so we are already being obedient.

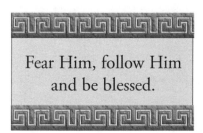

Fear Him, follow Him and be blessed.

Second, we should have a delightful attitude when following God's commands. We should not walk around moping and pouting because God has ordered us to do certain things. Why? Because we were first blessed! I tried in vain to keep sleeping when the Lord put this column on my heart, but my body kept shaking and twitching. Roland wanted to get some rest at 4:22 a.m., but the Lord wanted me to get up and upload what He was downloading into my spirit. My blessing was having that bed to sleep in, breath in my body and a forum to share such good news! How childish of us to already be blessed through association with him and then grow despondent because we are to follow his commands, whatever and whenever they are given.

I recall it like it was yesterday, when I came home from college to discover the door to one of my sisters' room was off the hinges. I asked my sister, LeVita, what happened, and she said that my sister, Kenya, had the audacity to tell my dad that LeVita's room was her room. He quickly proceeded to remove the door from its hinges and instructed her to get dressed and sleep with an open doorway. You might find his actions harsh, but he was showing her that as long as she lived under his roof it was his house and she was to follow his commands. Stay with me, I'm going somewhere.

There were countless other times when my dad told me to do something and it didn't quite jive with what I had planned. Yet I remained the dutiful son because he was my father and I was in his house, what he said was the law and I was to follow his commands. As long as I lived in his house I was clothed. As long as I lived in his house I had food to eat. As long as I lived in his house, I was provided for when I needed something for school. As long as I lived in his house, no one from the outside could harm me because my daddy had my back.

Now go back to Psalms 111 and 112. When a blessed man first fears the Lord, and finds delight in his commands, "his children will be mighty in the land; the generation of the upright will be blessed. Wealth and riches are in his house, and his righteousness endures forever. Even in darkness light dawns for the upright, for the gracious and compassionate and righteous man. Good will come to him who is generous and lends freely, who conducts his affairs with justice. Surely he will never be shaken; a righteous man will be remembered forever. He will have no fear of bad news; his heart is steadfast, trusting in the Lord. His heart is secure, he will have no fear; in the end he will look in triumph on his foes. He has scattered abroad his gifts to the poor, his righteousness endures forever; his horn will be lifted high in honor."

Talk about a blessing! All of that is possible, but first we have to fear the Lord.

I can say that blessings have come my way by virtue of following the commands of my father and mother. Yes, he is an earthly being who has made mistakes and will continue to do so. But there is little doubt that God has instilled in him a heart that is focused on guiding and steering his wife and five children. I can't sit here and do the things I do in media without realizing that had I not paid attention to his commands when it came to reading and writing (and watching five hours of news a day, even when I didn't like it!) there is no way I could have been a successful journalist.. My inability to crack under peer pressure is directly related to the discipline and leadership skills he and my mother instilled in me. As a result, what God has taught him, which was passed on to me and my brother and three sisters, will last from one generation to the next by virtue of him being obedient to the Lord.

Now is the time for more men and women, especially men, to be like Reginald L. Martin Sr., and instill fear in their children. A child should see you as a loving and caring figure, but at the same time know that you cannot be crossed for fear of having to pay the price. The Lord often punished Israel for not paying attention to his commands. Yes, He loved them and showed them compassion time and time again, but He could not allow them to escape punishment for doing wrong in His eyes.

As you go forward in your daily life, understand that we are to have fear of the Lord. We should never possess a casual attitude towards God and think that we can knowingly sin and do wrong, and then lean on His grace, mercy and understanding. I knew that my daddy would be there for me when I messed up, but I didn't want to put him in a position of having to bail me out time after time. If I simply followed his directions first, I wouldn't be in that position. The same goes for each and every one of us when it comes to our relationship with our heavenly father.

# Thank God
# for Daddy

*Text focus: 2 Samuel 9:1-13*

***

If there were one moment that dramatically changed my life, it would certainly be the decision to attend the 1989 national convention of the National Association of Black Journalists.

The convention was being held in New York City during August, and several months earlier I had attended the NABJ Region 7 conference in Little Rock, Arkansas. A group of students from Texas A&M University drove up to New York City in vans, excited about attending the regional gathering of the world's largest minority media organization.

After listening to a variety of speakers talk about the importance of the organization, I decided to run for the student representative's seat on the NABJ national board. I certainly had some ideas on how we could improve the lot of students, and felt I could represent us well as only the second student to serve on the board. But by the time the convention was rolling around, my money was funny.

The cost to attend the national convention would exceed $1,000 when you included hotel, airfare, registration and expenses. At the time I was a college sophomore, my brother was heading into his junior year at A&M and my sister was enrolling in Aggieland for her freshman year. Three children in college at one time was certainly a tough predicament for my parents, and the thought of spending $1,000 was non-existent.

As luck would have it (I say it was the Lord), our chapter sent letters out to 31 foundations in Texas seeking support to attend the convention. We received 30 rejection letters. That one letter came from the Strake Foundation and included a check for $1,000, which went towards two hotel rooms for eight students.

The foundation was headed by George Strake Jr., a prominent Houston businessman and former chairman of the Texas Republican Party. We became friends after George visited my eleventh grade government class in 1986, and I proceeded to pepper him with questions on a variety specific policies from the Reagan Administration. George was startled by the depth of my questions (Hey, I was attending Jack Yates' Magnet School of Communications!) and we immediately began a dialogue that continued through college. Praise the Lord for that meeting because we needed the dough!

But I still faced a problem with transportation, which couldn't be solved by the $1,000 donation.

During this time my dad was seriously looking to switch jobs. He had been working for the national rail company, Amtrak, and was close to leaving.

I told my mom how important it was that I attend the convention, and she told me to speak to my father.

The next day, I was sitting at our kitchen table when my dad came in to ask me about the convention. The job he was close to taking would pay more than his current job (it was also more hazardous) and with three kids in college and two others at home, the additional income would have been nice.

"So how important is it that you attend this conference?" he asked.

"Daddy, if I win this position, it could change my life and lay the groundwork for my future as a journalist," I said.

He looked at me with a deep, probing look, and I tried to convey as hard as I could through the look on my face that it was critical for me to attend the convention.

A week or so later he said he wasn't taking the job.

Why was this such a big deal? Because as the child of an Amtrak employee, I could ride the train for free. Even though it was a two-day ride from Houston to New York City, it would get me to the city and allow me to attend the convention.

I can't tell you how thrilled I was with his decision. I knew that the new job could have meant more money, but it was absolutely critical that I attend the NABJ national convention.

When August rolled around, my sister and I boarded the train for our journey to New York City. While in the city, she stayed at my uncle's house on Long Island while I got to hob-knob with some of the nation's top black journalists.

As fate would have it, I did win the student representative's position, which allowed me to serve two years on the board of directors. My leadership in the position during those two years paved the way for me to establish relationships with individuals who had a direct effect on my career.

The recommendation for my first job at the *Austin American-Statesman* came from Don Flores, then a publisher in El Paso and the president of the National Association of Hispanic Journalists. He told me to apply in Austin, and called Drew Marcks to recommend them hiring me. They did.

At the same time Don was pushing me to Austin, Ken Bunting, then assistant managing editor at the *Fort Worth Star-Telegram*, was interviewing me. I didn't get hired because the *Dallas Times Herald* shut down right before my graduation, flooding the market with more experienced journalists. But in 1993, he hired me as city hall reporter. When did we first meet? At that 1989 NABJ convention.

In 2000, Roy Johnson left *Sports Illustrated* to become editorial director of Vanguarde Media, and editor-in-chief of *Savoy* Magazine, a lifestyles publication for African Americans that he conceived while working at Time Inc. Roy wanted me to come to New York to work as news editor, but I preferred to stay in Dallas. He hired me anyway (of course, at a much lower salary!) and that resulted in my first job for a national magazine. That relationship was forged at multiple NABJ conventions, but first in 1989.

The next year, I called one of my former board members and told him about an idea I had to launch a black news and information website. Unbeknownst to me, Neil Foote had been lured away from the Belo Corporation by Tom Joyner to launch a site called BlackAmericaWeb.com. When BAW actually launched in June 2001, Neil called me and said, "I want you as the editor." Again, that job was a direct benefit of the relationships established through NABJ.

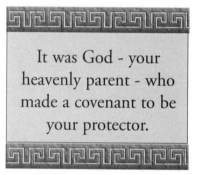

It was God - your heavenly parent - who made a covenant to be your protector.

I can go on and on and on about how a single sacrificial decision in 1989 by my dad, to stay on his job and allow me to travel for free to a convention, has paid dividends for me ever since. What many of us have to understand is that there are some decisions by our parents — known and unknown — that have a tremendous impact on our lives.

Many of us think that we have achieved success in life because of how hard we've worked in school and at work, yet we forget that it was on the backs of mothers, fathers, grandparents, uncles and aunts that led us to enjoy those fruits. In an age where children seem to blame their parents for all that's wrong with their life, all of us should step back and thank momma and daddy for the personal sacrifices they made to improve our lives.

I can say that without a doubt, Mephibosheth did just that.

Here was a man who as a child, was crippled (2 Samuel 4:4), thereby forced to depend on others for the rest of his life.

Mephibosheth was the son of a future king (Johnathan, his father, was Saul's first born), and clearly taken care of. But the Bible records in 1 Samuel 31 show that Johnathan was killed in battle. Then his father, Saul, took his own life instead of allowing his enemies to kill him.

Imagine Mephibosheth's state of mind. His provider — dad and granddad— are both gone, and the man who his grandfather tried to kill several times, David, is now the king. There is little doubt he was scared.

But there was something that Mephibosheth was not aware of, his father had so much love and affection for David that he chose to give up his right to the throne in order for David to ascend as king (1 Samuel 18:1-4). In doing so, Johnathan protected David on numerous occasions from being killed by Saul (1 Samuel 19:1-7; 1 Samuel 20). It was during one of those occasions that Johnathan, being the dutiful father that he was, established a covenant with David.

*"Show me unfailing kindness like that of the LORD as long as I live, so that I may not be killed, and do not ever cut off your kindness from my family-not even when the LORD has cut off every one of David's enemies from the face of the earth."* (NIV)

Johnathan knew the dangers he faced. He understood that either David would get killed or he would possibly die since he fought at the side of his father. So Johnathan was smart enough to protect his children and spiritually cover them by entering into the covenant with David. That's a biblical example of a father serving as priest, protector and provider for his family. He was *"one in spirit with David"* (1 Samuel 18:1-4) and recognized that God chose David; he protected the life of David, which in turn meant that his family would be provided for in the case of his demise.

As a result, Mephibosheth got the chance to sit at the king's table, have all of the land that Saul owned returned to his care, and taken care of by the family who looked after Saul.

Boy, did Johnathan hook his son up!

Now I'm sure there is someone who is reading this and is saying, "That's great. Your dad did the right thing by staying on a job. That free ticket helped you in your career, and Mephibosheth was taken care of because of an unknown promise made by his father. But my dad (or mom) treated me with disrespect. In fact, he was an absentee father who made my life and that of my siblings a living hell. I wish I had someone who looked after me and my well-being so I could enjoy this life."

I fully understand and appreciate your feelings and how you don't have a "what-my-parent" did for me story. It is wrong and pathetic when men serve as sperm donors instead of fathers and husbands. It is terrible when some females are not Proverbs 31 women who look after their families with care and tenderness. Some of you have been abandoned, verbally or sexually abused, and left for dead by a sorry parent. Those are feelings and circumstances that are hard to get over. But I have one word that can heal you of those angry feelings: Jesus.

Take the time to look at this situation from another perspective. While your biological father or mother made your life a living hell, the fact is you are still standing. That's right. I want you to go to a mirror and look at yourself. What do you see? A child of God who had to contend with adversity from their biological and worldly parents, but who was looked after and cared for by your spiritual father.

It was God — your heavenly parent — who made a covenant to be your protector. You were taken through hell and back, but the fact that you are still here is a testament to your intestinal fortitude and the reality that God has a purpose for your life. God didn't want you to be sexually abused, but you can conquer that situation and be a vessel to bless someone else. The Lord didn't want you to have to scrap for food as a child, yet today you can look back on that situation and know that you survived and you are thriving today.

Our Lord chose to send his son to earth in order to establish a covenant to die for our sins. God offered up his Son as a living sacrifice for each and every one of us. Just like Mephibosheth, we weren't around when the covenant was established. But Mephibosheth got to reap the rewards of his dad's covenant. The same goes for us. We are reaping the rewards for the covenant established by God to sacrifice His sins for every one of us.

I make it my mission to publicly thank my dad and mom for the sacrifices they made for my brothers and sisters. And yes, I thank God for providing me with Godly parents.

Why don't you join me in sending up shouts of 'Amen!' and 'Hallelujah!' to our Lord and savior, Jesus Christ, for being the nurturing, loving and sacrificial God that he is?

There is no doubt that I'm better off for that decision by my dad in August 1989. Mephibosheth was better off because of the covenant his dad entered into with David. And all of us are better off for what took place at Calvary.

# The real meaning of the prayer of Jabez

*Text focus: 1 Chronicles 4:9-10*

\*\*\*

There were few books in 2001 that caused more of a stir than Bruce Wilkinson's The *Prayer of Jabez*.

Focusing on a small and often overlooked prayer in 1 Chronicles 4, Wilkinson captured the imagination of the world, selling as many as 100,000 copies a week and residing at the top of the *New York Times* Best Sellers list for months. The book was considered a must-read in Bible study groups, churches and by pastors near and far. It also became something of a cottage industry for Wilkinson, complete with a *Jabez* diary, workbook, pens, *Jabez* prayer books for teens and children and other ministerial accessories.

My wife, Jacquie, an ordained minister who was blessed tremendously by the encouraging words offered in the small but powerful book, introduced me to the book.

Yet as I listened to so many people discussed The *Prayer of Jabez*, a dangerous trend began to emerge. Instead of delving deeper into the understanding and the purpose Wilkinson had for the book by uncovering the power of the prayer, many people chose to treat it as a personal prayer for wealth and material possessions.

The *Prayer of Jabez* all of a sudden became a get-rich-book, similar to those offered in the money section of the bookstore.

A few years ago during an interview with the Rev. Kirbyjon Caldwell, who was promoting his book, *The Gospel of Good Success*, he criticized the perspective of many Christians who have begun to look towards God as a "spiritual slot machine."

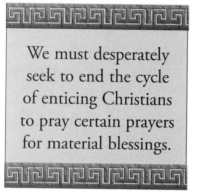

We must desperately seek to end the cycle of enticing Christians to pray certain prayers for material blessings.

According to Caldwell's critique, any time we need to get out of a jam, crave a new job, want a new car, house, husband, wife or baby, we simply go to God, pray earnestly, and recite Psalms 37:4 over and over, *"Delight yourself in the Lord, and he will give you the desires of your heart."* Then we simply sit back and wait for God to show up and show out. Caldwell definitely believes that God can and will provide...if it's His will to do so.

Flip back to Psalms 37:1 and read the conditions that God has established in order to give us the desires of our heart.

Now, how many times have you heard someone say: "I'm doing right and he/she has dates all the time, is driving a big car and has a nice house, yet I'm stuck where I am."

Amazing. Christians doing the right thing (as instructed in Psalms 47: 3) are envious of those who aren't, and are craving those materials goods they possess. So which would you prefer? The blessings of righteous living — spiritual prosperity — or those material goods that, according to 47:2, *"Will soon wither, like green plants they will soon die away."*

Keep in mind that we are not seeking our will, but God's will. It is foolish to continue to pray for what you want if you've never taken the time to go to God and ask, "What do you want?" Even the Lord's Prayer tells us that "thy kingdom come; thy will be done."

All of the accoutrements of life don't mean a thing if we don't have a spirit that is focused on our relationship with Christ. When you study and pray the prayer of Jabez, it is not merely a prayer meant to increase your bank account, stock portfolio or the size of your house. We should be seeking God to "bless me and enlarge my territory!" for the Lord.

Wilkinson recounted his saying of the prayer and how God expanded the territory of his ministry. Yes, he discussed how praying the prayer led financial barriers to come down so he could do God's work. But the selfish motive of personal wealth building is not the true purpose of prayer.

How many of you who have prayed the prayer of Jabez or read the book just to ask God to bless you and increase your territory to do His work? That may mean witnessing to others, discipling young men or women or using your spiritual gift of intercession to pray on behalf of others.

We must desperately seek to end the cycle of enticing Christians to pray certain prayers for material blessings. If God chooses to do so, that's wonderful. But when we reduce God to a spiritual check writer, we deny the true purpose he has for us, and ultimately, his power.

# Thank God for
# the Mama Baileys
# of the world

W hen kids are asked who they want to be like when they grow up, the usual names are rattled off: Oprah Winfrey, Bill Gates, the President of the United States, Michael Jordan or Tiger Woods. We never hear a child say, "I want to be like Mama Bailey."

I first came across this wonderful woman of God in 2002 while visiting the Inspiring Body of Christ in Dallas. On the Sunday my wife and I visited, the Rev. Rickie Rush, the pastor of the church, recognized Mama Bailey as the church's Member of the Year.

It was fascinating to find out what made this woman so special that the pastor would choose her out of nearly 5,000 members, and recognize her with the honor. It didn't take me long to figure out why it was a no-brainer.

Mama Bailey is not a woman who runs a big-time corporation in the city. She doesn't walk around exerting her influence on public policy; she isn't on a first name basis with the mayor and a few members of Congress or discovering great things in a medical lab. She is simply one of those discreet and silent saints who go about her business by helping people through the difficult moments of life.

Rev. Rush told the congregation that Mama Bailey doesn't even own a car and rarely has money in her pocket, yet whenever there is a member of the church in the hospital, he will get there and find she is already there holding their hand and praying with them. When his own mother died, Mama Bailey didn't even ask whether his father needed help, she just went over and cooked him several meals and sat on the front porch, tending to his needs while he grieved over the loss of his wife. It was by her presence and giving spirit that his father finally came to church, something even the pastor couldn't do!

> She lived a prosperous life because she availed herself to the Lord and chose to do His will.

One woman stood up and said that when she lost her child through a miscarriage, she and her husband were distraught. Yet there was Mama Bailey, offering them a shoulder to cry on and providing them with comforting words and prayer.

And as these nice things were being said about her, Mama Bailey lay spread out on the altar, prostrating herself before the Lord and giving Him thanks for the gifts being bestowed upon her, including money, a TV/VCR, a shopping spree at a store and other goodies.

What was evident by the story of Mama Bailey wasn't all the great things she did, it was the simple fact that she lived a prosperous life because she availed herself to the Lord and chose to do His will. Rush said Bailey, who was retired, never fretted about money, a car or a big house. All she cared about was going where God sent her and doing what He commanded her.

Again, the material goods didn't matter; it was her spirit that was rich.

Far too many of us have come to the conclusion that a big home, expensive car and a big mutual fund make us prosperous. But that pales in comparison to the person who is smiling and joyous even when they only have a few dollars in the bank. To be spiritually prosperous means that I might not have the resources of a king, but the King of Kings has blessed me mightily with a spirit that wants for nothing but to be enveloped in the presence of the Holy Spirit.

If your money is tight, you can still be a blessing. Speak a kind word to someone. Pray for your neighbor. If you can't afford to send flowers to someone in the hospital, just visit them and sit with them. If your niece or nephew is graduating from high school and you can't buy them a gift, offer them salvation before they go to college. That is a gift that can't be measured monetarily.

The next time you hear someone talk of spiritual prosperity, tell him or her the story of Mama Bailey.

If any of us ever wonder what it means to be spiritually prosperous, all we have to do is think of Mama Bailey and her work for the Lord. It truly is more important than what most of us are driving ourselves to accomplish.

# Don't just thank God, represent Him

*Text focus: Romans 12:1*
***

There Sean "P. Diddy" or "Puff Daddy" or "Whatever-the-heck-we're-calling-him-this-week" Combs stood: wearing his trademark shades, a diamond-crusted cross resting on his bare chest (his shirt unbutton down his navel), thanking God for being able to co-host the American Music Awards in 2002 because he was in a courtroom on trial for weapons charges.

Combs should have been giving God all the glory. He got off, his former gal pal Jennifer Lopez wasn't tried, but his protégé, Shyne, got 10 years for shooting up a New York nightclub.

My issue isn't with Combs thanking God — I believe God should get continuous praise each and every single day. But wouldn't it be nice to see entertainers and celebrities not only continue to thank God, but represent him?

It is tiresome to hear Destiny's Child throw God's name all over the place, but put out a song called "Bootylicious."

"I don't think you ready for this jelly; I don't think you ready for this jelly; I don't think you ready for this; 'Cos my body too bootylicious for ya babe."

Yeah, right! Those are not the words young Christian ladies should use to glorify God.

Combs was willing to thank God, yet a few months before the ceremony he chose to be the centerpiece of a cover story in *Details* magazine, surrounded by butt-naked women. I don't recall P. Diddy giving God the glory then.

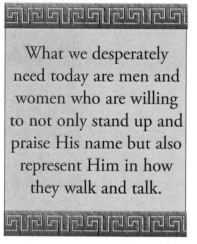

What we desperately need today are men and women who are willing to not only stand up and praise His name but also represent Him in how they walk and talk.

Some would suggest that the critique of such shallow behavior is judgmental. I'm sure the e-mails will come flying in that my position is one rooted in jealousy or the attempt for one set of Christian values to prevail over another. It's not. The issue is simple: God should not be pimped when we want to give Him thanks for winning an award. Instead of yelling His name, we should make an effort to represent Him in our walk.

Every single one of us is a sinner. There is no disputing that. But if we choose to walk in the way of the Lord, then we must carry ourselves as such. If we want to represent ourselves as believers in the body of Christ, don't you think we ought to be extremely careful about all of the body we choose to flash to the general public?

It is difficult for those in the entertainment industry to withstand the pressure to sing songs filled with sexual lyrics, produce videos that involve gyrating women or wear outrageous outfits that leave nothing to the imagination. But by not "conforming to this world" (Romans 12:2) we should work to "transform" the world by saying, *"No, I'm not going to do it that way.*

*If God has put me in this position to use my talents, I don't have to compromise who I am for the sake of a dollar."*

What we desperately need today are men and women who are willing to not only stand up and praise His name but also represent Him in how they walk and talk.

# Don't just thank God, represent Him

On that same American Music Awards stage, Yolanda Adams won the award from Contemporary Gospel Artist of the year. Looking lovely as all get out, Adams didn't sacrifice her morality by to dressing like Lil' Kim. Instead, she kept her integrity and allowed her light to shine through her body and clothes as opposed to having all of the lights on her. When she accepted her award, Adams didn't just thank God for the blessings, she spoke of the need to follow Him and live in His will each and every single day.

I know her speech wasn't what many wanted to hear — heck, Snoop Dogg was sitting on the front row with Bishop Don "Magic" Juan, a pimp made famous by his role in the movie, *American Pimp* — but it was desperately needed in a place filled with hero-worshipping and decadence.

As a member of the media, I know first-hand of the power of words and images. That's why it would be wonderful to see artists like Combs or Destiny's Child use their enormous media access to match their actions with their rhetoric. Then let's see young brothers and sisters emulate that instead of the bling-bling lifestyle.

# Remembering the Sabbath is rare these days

*Text focus: Exodus 20:8*
***

Whenever overtime slots open up on a Sunday, it's not rare to see several people vying for those precious dollars.

When I was about 12 or 13 years old, my uncle Carl wanted to cut my grandfather's grass. That sounded like a good idea to me, a son wanting to help his elderly father.

But Poppa didn't want any of that. He made it clear in no uncertain terms that there would be no work in his house on Sunday, the day he reserved for praying, relaxing and cooling out with family.

I suppose if Poppa were still alive, he would be proud of Eli Herring.

Herring was a 6-foot-8, 335-pound Brigham Young lineman and likely first or second-round National Football League pick in the 1995 draft, who wrote a letter to every NFL general manager requesting that he not be drafted.

Why? Because he was a devout Mormon who takes seriously his religion's teaching not to work on Sunday, the Sabbath day.

And as we all know, between September and January, Sunday has become the day on which professional football players strap on their pads and helmets for the enjoyment of fans across the globe.

Herring's actions run counter to most, if not all, college seniors and juniors, who have feverishly worked out a coveted spot on a professional football team. Players and their agents write letters, make videos or anything else possible to get NFL executives to notice the players and their athletic talents.

But Herring wanted no part of the charade. Instead, he prepared to become a high school math teacher or high school football or track coach.

"It was a tough decision," he told the Associated Press. "I've thought about playing pro football since I was a kid. But NFL games are on Sunday, and as I was growing up my family always recognized Sunday as the Sabbath. For me, personally, it just wouldn't be right."

It's not uncommon for other Mormons to show their athletic prowess on Sunday. San Francisco 49ers quarterback and Hall of Famer Steve Young didn't let his religion get in the way of playing, nor did Gifford Nielsen, now a Houston sportscaster who logged several years as a backup quarterback in Houston.

Even Herring's teammate, John Walsh, left college after his junior year for the fame and fortune of the NFL.

"When I was making my decision, everyone brought up Steve Young as being a guy who has been a good influence for the church through the fame he's received in the NFL," Herring recalled. "He has been a good example for the church, but for me, [playing on Sunday] isn't an option."

It seems as if the idea of reserving Sunday as a day to pray and play has been lost on a society always looking to wring a few more hours out of our tired bodies.

Ever heard of the phrase, "Thank God it's Friday?"

Yet when the weekend finally arrives, many of us find some reason to come into the office or hit our home computer just to take care of a few items.

Whenever overtime slots open up on a Sunday, it's not rare to see several people vying for those precious dollars.

Up until the 1980s, Texas abided by the old Blue Laws, which prohibited malls and other businesses from being open on Sundays.

I remember a lot of people saying that it was blasphemous for stores to milk every last penny out of shoppers by being open on Sunday. People were crying and carrying on about how we don't respect the religions that many of us claim to practice.

And what happened? Many of those same complainers now are the first ones out of church, trying to beat the crowds to the mall.

We all have our own reasons for doing the things that we do, and it is not wrong for people to work on Sunday. Many are diligently working to get ahead and up the career ladder as fast as we can.

But there comes a time when we must consider our priorities.

Should spending time with our families take precedence over finishing that report for the boss? Is it so important to pick up that dress or tie at the mall that I can't pay a visit to a friend in the hospital?

I guess we all should say, "Thank God for Eli Herring."

Sometimes we all need a gentle reminder to make us remember what is important in life.

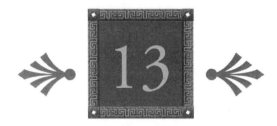

# A spiritual lesson
# from Sex in the City

*Text focus: Matthew 19:11-12 (The Message)*
\*\*\*

Shakespeare once said that there were sermons in stones, and after watching an episode of HBO's racy and comical *Sex in the City*, I couldn't agree more with the popular playwright.

For those of you who aren't avid watchers of the show — get real my holier than thou Christian compadres, you know there are shows, programs that others object to, that you can't miss — it is told through the eyes of Carrie, a single New York City columnist who traverses the city, along with her three female friends, in search of that elusive meaningful relationship (or the occasional quickie, hence the name of the show).

In this episode, Aidan, Carrie's beau, asks her to marry him. But in her fiercely independent way, she doesn't want to flash the ring on her hand.

Instead, she allows it to dangle from her necklace.

Carrie's feeling okay about this marriage thing and agrees to try on a wedding dress with her friend, Amanda. As they laugh at the hideous dresses they don, Carrie begins to develop a rash on her body as she begins to think about the prospects of marriage — one man, one sexual partner, complete commitment. Forever.

She yells at Amanda to get the dress off her, who virtually rips it off.

Later in the day, Carrie tells Aidan that she doesn't want to get married now because she's a bit uncomfortable. He says that he's cool with that and is willing to wait, but later, as they walk past a gorgeously lit water fountain, he begins to press her to get married now.

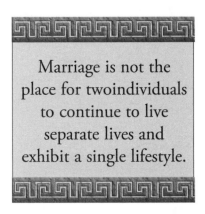

Marriage is not the place for twoindividuals to continue to live separate lives and exhibit a single lifestyle.

Carrie tells Aidan that she loves him, but she is not ready for that major commitment. What does he do? He throws a temper tantrum. They later sleep apart in their apartment, only to have Carrie announce that he moved out the next day.

I happened to catch the show while at Ohio University, where I was scheduled to give a speech the next day. Several of my Alpha Phi Alpha fraternity brothers invited me to visit their frat house, and we caught the show with several members of Alpha Kappa Alpha sorority. When the show concluded, several of the women began to howl that Carrie was nuts for not taking Aidan up on his offer.

But as I sat there and smiled, God began to speak to me and shared with me that despite all of the things that someone might find fault with Carrie's sexually charged single lifestyle, she was being honest and upholding a significant position on marriage.

We live in a society where so many people are getting married for love, but they don't have a full understanding of what is expected in marriage. Aidan said he loved Carrie and wanted to be with her for the rest of his life, yet he wasn't listening to the doubts she had about their budding union.

The Lord began to tell me that Carrie was objecting to marriage because she didn't want to establish a covenant between her, Aidan and the Lord, and not fulfill the responsibilities of marriage. She essentially fast-forwarded through the wedding and the marriage, to the inevitable divorce which was sown in her protestations prior to marriage.

I have long held that if an individual is willing to do 95 percent what is required of them in marriage, they should not do it because that 5 percent will kick their behind during the course of the marriage.

Marriage is one of the hardest things in this world to do. The Bible says that when man and woman — again, man and woman — unite in marriage, they are becoming "one" (Matthew 19:5). That doesn't mean that he no longer has a brain and she no longer has an opinion, but it signifies that from that moment on they are to act in unison and proceed as one. We all know that that is sometimes hard to do, but we are to strive for oneness at all times. That means the concept of your car-my car, your money-my money, your friends my friends, etc., should be left at the altar, along with your singleness.

Marriage is not the place for two individuals to continue to live separate lives and exhibit a single lifestyle. But all too often that happens. That's a roommate, not a wife or husband.

What Carrie saw above all else was that marriage is important, is sacred and there is a trust between the two that is unparalleled. We live in a world of contracts and legal definitions, but marriage is a covenant that has been established between man, woman and God. And we should know that a covenant is stronger than any contract.

That's why it is so painful when we go through a divorce.

If you are married and are going through tremendous difficulties, I want you to take out a pen and pad and begin to go on a self-journey to the time when you were single. What were your thoughts, feelings and positions on marriage? Were there any things that you made clear that you would or wouldn't do? What was your state of mind prior to marriage? How did you view your parents' marriage? What did you like and dislike? How have your past relationships formed your opinion of your spouse and the idea of marriage? Do you believe in pre-nuptial agreements? Did you see yourself as entering into oneness or simply having someone who could help you do stuff around the house with and vacation with? Do you and your intended spouse share the same spiritual views and moral values?

I know these may sound like simple questions, but they go to the heart of what may be troubling in your marriage. You or your spouse may not have placed a high premium on marriage like Carrie, and now you find yourself in a painful period where there seems to be no end in sight.

If you are single or engaged, you should do the same thing. It is imperative that you deal with yourself and your expectations before you choose to marry.

Marriage will bring out issues that have long been suppressed in your life. Intimacy. Love. Trust. Lack of affection from a father or mother. High expectations. You name it, marriage will cause the hidden areas of your life to be revealed and exposed. What you then do and how you handle it will determine whether you allow it to infect or strengthen your marriage.

Marriage is not the place for selfishness; it fosters selflessness. It encourages, supports and provides a comforting presence. But it can also be your personal mirror, causing you to look at issues in your life that may be uncomfortable.

It is an institution that requires those who are serious about it. In Matthew 19, Jesus said, using The Message translation, "*Not everyone is mature enough to live a married life. It requires a certain aptitude and grace. Marriage isn't for everyone...But if you're capable of growing into the largeness of marriage, do it.*"

If you are planning to get married and have doubts about whether you can fulfill the terms of your marriage, don't allow others to shrug it off as "cold feet." Take a personal assessment, and address those issues. The pain you encounter today for not taking a walk down the aisle, may save you the horrendous pain of walking down the corridor to divorce court.

# Shut up,
# get up and go

*Text Focus: John 5: 2-9. Emphasis is on verses 6, 7 and 8*

\*\*\*

Are there many things in this life worse than having to endure a pity party? Don't act like you are the holiest of holy. There has been at least one time or another where you have engaged in your own personal pity party, and if not, you were an invited guest to such a party.

There you are, sitting there, whining and carrying on about what you don't have, and what you could have had if this happened or if that happened.

My wife will tell you, if you want to have a pity party, please forget my address because I don't want that kind of an invitation!

Such a sad and demoralizing party came to mind while reading John 5 and the story of the man who had been ill for 38 years. I'll be that age in November, and I can't imagine being ill all of my life. But here was this man, sitting by the pool in Jerusalem where the sick, blind and lame went to wait on an angel to descend from heaven, touch the water and heal them.

But it seems that each and every time the angel would stir up the water (John 5:4) the ill man would be late and miss his blessing. Why? Because he was lying there and no one was willing to pick him up and put him in the pool. They were focused on getting their own healing and they didn't have time to worry about his affliction.

So one day Jesus comes walking up and asks the man a simple question: *"Do you wish to get well?"* (John 5:6). Now let's digress: the man had been lying there, sick for the last 38 years and the Messiah steps up and asks him a question that should only be met with one answer. But like a man stuck in his own pity party, he chose to whine.

> We must discover for ourselves that we are standing before, and have access to, the One that can solve any problem.

*"Sir, I have no man to put me into the pool when the water is stirred up, but while I am coming, another steps down before me."* (John 5:7)

Using your sanctified imagination, just close your eyes and imagine what was going through Jesus' mind. "What in the world is this man talking about? Here I am trying to help him and all I get to hear about is how sick he is and how no one is willing to help him and how he is to slow to get his healing and how someone steps in front of him." Jesus may not have done this, but I'm confident that if it was you or me, we would be rolling our eyes and looking at our friends (disciples) and say, "Did I ask to hear all of that?"

Luckily, Jesus didn't respond that way.

*"Get up! Pick up your mat and walk"* (John 5:8). With that command, the man was healed without even having to touch the water.

It dawned on me how this crippled man had been sucked into a pity party that clearly was 38 years in the making. Granted, he didn't know who Jesus was when he walked up, but Jesus did have the common sense to ask: "Do you wish to get well?" The answer should have been a resounding yes! But instead, the man chose to spin his boring and pitiful story about how he can't do this or do that.

Does this sound like you? Are you going through something that has been a burden on your soul for a long time, and all you ever find yourself doing is talking and talking about how bad your situation is? Again, put your holiness aside and just be honest: are you like that ill man by the pool? Has Jesus or one of his angels (friend, family or church member) come to you and asked if you wanted to be healed, but had your focus on the wrong thing, and all you did was concentrate on your dilemma, not the answer to your prayers?

That is one of the biggest issues Christians have, our faith is so weak at times when we are presented with the answer to our cares and concerns — Jesus Christ. Yet we don't answer in the affirmative when we are asked if we want a healing.

Marriages are in disrepair; children are losing their minds; pastors are facing temptation after temptation; we are catching mucho hell on the job; our brothers and sisters are jealous of our success; and all we have time to do when we go to the altar and ask for a healing from God is to respond with a bunch of problems.

In order to escape our personal pity party, we must discover for ourselves that we are standing before and have access to the One that can solve any problem, heal any wound, or close any door and open another. What we have to do is know how to answer Him.

God does not need to know our problem; He already knows what we think. Read John 5:6 again: "When Jesus saw him lying there, and knew that he had already been a long time in that condition, He said to him, '*Do you wish to get well?*'" Even before Jesus asked him a question he knew his problem. And the same goes for you. God already knows what heavy yoke you are carrying. So don't waste your golden opportunity by telling him what is bugging you. Answer his probing question with a loud statement: "Yes, God! I'm ready to be healed!"

# It pays to
# be different

*Text focus: Numbers 13-14*
***

My daddy always made a point to tell his five children not to follow the crowd because that could lead to trouble and ruin. Peer pressure is such a destructive thing in our society, and the "go along" attitude has led to many negative results that can sometimes have lifelong consequences.

This point is driven home in Numbers 13. Moses had already led his people of out of bondage in Israel, and the Lord was clearing their path to the promise land. God told Moses to send some men to Canaan to explore the land and report back what they saw. Moses didn't want a quick and easy report; he specifically asked for the strengths and weaknesses (v. 18), and the condition of the land, soil and trees. In 40 days the men did as ordered, including cutting off a cluster of grapes as evidence of what they saw with their own eyes.

When they returned, the report was going along fine. They affirmed that just as the Lord said, the land was flowing with milk and honey, and there was fruit. Then they got the bright idea to stray from what they were told and they began to remark about how strong and powerful the people were and how fortified their cities were.

At that point, Caleb got sick and tired of the nonsense and cut right to the chase, "We should go up and take possession of the land, for we can certainly do it." But the other men continued, scaring the Israelites into thinking the people were "of great size" and standing next to them, they "seemed like grasshoppers."

Now that was the last thing the Israelites needed. You do remember that these were the same folks who drove Moses mad with all of their complaining about the lack of food? In fact, as a result of their disobedience, Moses couldn't cross into the Promise Land. So they began to hem and haw, crying and complaining about how crazy Moses was for leading them out of Egypt and how they were going to die in the desert.

God will bless us for not following the crowd and staying on the path of righteousness.

Angry at their reaction to the false stories from Canaan, Moses and Aaron fell facedown and began to prayer. Even Caleb and Joshua dropped to their knees; they clearly understood how the Israelites had angered God. Cleary upset by their actions, the Lord appeared and began to rebuke the Israelites for their outright disobedience. As a result, the Lord struck down all of the men who caused the grumbling, but he spared Joshua and Caleb.

Use your sanctified imagination and visualize Joshua and Caleb patting one another on the back and saying with a sense of relief, "Man, I'm sure glad we didn't act a fool and follow those fools. We would be dead now."

Joshua and Caleb offer us a wonderful lesson about how God will bless us for not following the crowd and staying on the path of righteousness. It would have been easy for the two of them to remain quiet, but instead they quickly spoke up and pleaded with the Israelites to ignore the other men.

Unfortunately, their pleadings were to no avail. In fact, scripture says that the whole assembly talked about stoning the two of them!

There is no doubt that when we follow the calling of God, there will be some people who are not happy with what we have to say. They may be so angered that they will threaten you if you tell the truth, the whole truth and nothing but the truth. Many of our children in school remain silent when they see wrongdoing for fear of not being accepted by their friends. They are willing to risk remaining in the clique, rather than report someone who is using drugs, cheating or stealing.

But grownups do the same thing. Many people at Enron, Worldcom, Adelphia and other Fortune 500 companies that bit the dust in the last couple of years knew about the accounting scandals going on. But for fear of losing their jobs and upsetting co-workers, they chose to remain silent and turn the other way. The result? The companies crumbled because of the accounting irregularities, and thousands of people lost their entire savings and jobs as a result. Even those who remained silent lost their jobs, lost their incomes, and in some cases, went to prison.

A failure to speak up forcefully also contributed to the loss of two space shuttles — Columbia and Challenger. NASA higher-ups didn't want to listen to the folks who expressed concern about the O-rings in the case of Challenger, and later the debris damage to Columbia. The result? Both crews were killed and their families are now without fathers, mothers, husbands and wives.

Those of us in the kingdom must dare to be different. No longer should we sit by while others do all the talking. Our "friends" may not be standing behind us when we stand on truth, but I'm confident we will be blessed and spared by virtue of our decision. And even if doing the right thing means losing a job or a friend, we can know that we did what was right.

The next time you are faced with a critical decision to follow the crowd or follow the Lord, don't just remember Caleb and Jonathan. Think back on the consequences that fell on those who didn't do what they did.

# Spiritual Warfare: Trusting God to fight the battles of life

*Text focus: Ephesians 6*
***

There is nothing like praising God for His awesome and wonderful spirit.

During a three-month stay in Atlanta in 2000, I encountered a difficult and troubling week. But instead of escaping the madness by running and partying all weekend, I made the decision to sit down in my hotel room and stay entrenched in the Word by praying, meditating, praising, worshipping and simply sit and live in the presence of God.

How many times have you done that? I mean, no friends, no family, no phone calls (okay, just a couple); only the time where it's just you and God spending time together as He ministers to your spirit?

It was a difficult week where I had to encounter many people who didn''t want God's business to be done. It was backstabbing at its finest. Difficult in the sense where my credibility, integrity and patience was tested to the limit.

Although I knew it would be rough because the devil's imps had already shown themselves, it still was a test.

I had to ask myself and be honest with God and shout out, "Lord, you sent me here. You placed me here. So if this is your will, why in the hell is all of this going on?"

The Lord, in His own way, replied, "I never said it would be easy. But you have to trust me that I will bring you through the battle and the storm and put you on top when it is all said and done."

"Yea, that's nice and wonderful," I replied, "but that ain't doing much for me right now and I am getting my butt kicked; I have oiled my adversaries down; I have oiled their workspaces down; I have prayed them away and prayed their evil spirits away, but I still don't feel much relief."

God then took me to Ephesians 6 to remind me that when we are faced with difficulties, be it work, family, friends, financial difficulties or any other Goliath that we encounter, we must be steeped in the Word. I went to the New International Version of the Bible, but God led me to Eugene Peterson's Bible translation, *The Message*.

Here is what it says: "God is strong and wants to make you strong. So take everything the Master has set out for you, well-made weapons of the best materials. And put them to use so you will be able to stand up to everything the devil throws your way. This is no afternoon athletic contest that we'll walk away from and forget about in a couple of hours. This is for keeps, a life or-death fight to the finish against the devil and all his angels.

"Be prepared. You're up against far more than you can handle on your own. Take all the help you can get, every weapon God has issued, so that when it's all over but the shouting you'll still be on your felt. Truth, righteousness, peace, faith and salvation are more than words. God's Word is an indispensable weapon. In the same way, prayer is essential in this ongoing warfare. Pray hard and long. Pray for your brothers and sisters. Keep your eyes open. Keep each other"'s spirits up so that no one falls behind or drops out."

Did you see what was said at the end? GOD'S WORD IS AN INDISPENSABLE WEAPON. Talk about a line to make you shout!

See, regardless of where we are in our spiritual walk, we must continue to be engrossed in the Word so we are able to battle those things that come our way. It's very easy to praise and worship God while we are in good times, but our true faith comes to the surface when we are faced with a situation that seems hopeless, endless and seems as if it will crush us. But it is at that time that God says, "Job well done."

So many of us are going through difficult times right now, and it's made more difficult when we don't even know there is a war going on around us.

As a result, we are unprepared and caught off guard in the middle of the storm.

As Bishop Eddie L. Long of Atlanta's New Birth Missionary Baptist Church said during one of my visits to his church, "God has already handled that situation for you and you don't even know it. He has handled what your flesh has been trying to work out."

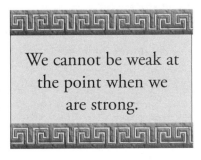

We cannot be weak at the point when we are strong.

Look, I'm human just like you. I can sit here and worry and try to think myself out of a situation, but there are some things that my flesh cannot handle, and that is where God allows His awesome power to step in and deal with it. We must continue to live and stay within the Word in order to gain our fill of His grace and mercy, no matter what's going on. "*Righteousness exalts a nation, but sin is a disgrace to any nation,*" says Proverbs 14:34 (NIV). *The Message* says: "*God's devotion makes a country strong; God avoidance leaves people weak.*"

We cannot be weak at the point when we are strong. But what always happens is that when we are at our weakest God is at his strongest. When we stand before him we are weak and meek, but when God has finished teaching, preaching, healing, molding and helping us, we must be strong and stand up to those forces we contend with.

Take delight in 2 Corinthians 12:9: "*But he said to me, 'My graced is sufficient for you, for my power is made perfect in weakness.' Therefore I will boast all the more gladly about my weaknesses, so that Christ's power may rest on me. That is why, for Christ's sake, I delight in weaknesses, in insults, in hardships, in persecutions, in difficulties. For when I am weak, then I am strong.'*"

I encourage each one of you to continue your daily reading and mediation. It is in those times that God continues to speak to us and encourage us and strengthen us.

*"Let me live that I may praise you, and may your laws sustain me, I have strayed like a lost sheep. Seek your servant, for I have not forgotten your commands,"* says Psalms 119:175-176.

Another verse to chew on is Psalms 147:5: *"Great is our Lord and mighty in power; his understanding has no limit."*

The power that resides in us is so awesome, allowing us to handle anything that comes our way. When we think something is over — job, marriage, a relationship with siblings and parents — the power of the Holy Spirit overtakes us and reminds us that all is not lost, and says, "I can handle it all, even as I handle the problems of Jimmy, Tonya, Bill, Carol, David and on and on and on."

The "I" is the great "I Am."

# Spiritual Warfare:
# Stay prepared for
# life's battles

*Text focus: Nehemiah 4:15-23*

\*\*\*

Former Oklahoma Sooners head coach Barry Switzer was once asked whether he worried about an opposing team's plan to stop his vaunted wishbone offense. The in-your-face Switzer simply said that it didn't matter; if his team ran their offense to perfection, there was nothing the defense could do to stop them.

Switzer was called a cocky and arrogant coach by many in the profession, yet no one could argue with the conference titles and national championships he won in building Oklahoma into a national powerhouse. What made Switzer so effective was that he didn't worry about what his opponent did; his efforts were concentrated on preparing his team and pushing them towards perfection.

That story flashed across my mind while reading Nehemiah 4:15-23. The people of Israel were trying to rebuild the wall around Jerusalem and they were facing fierce competition. Frustrated, tired and weary, they could have easily given up and remained at the mercy of their enemies. But under "Coach" Nehemiah, they were instructed that they were engaged in spiritual warfare and that they should keep working around the clock, while at the same time looking out for their enemies.

Nehemiah wasn't one of those guys who would say, "Oh, the Lord will provide," and then do nothing. No, he was given a plan by the Almighty to rebuild, but also knew that his followers would have to continue to fight if they would be successful.

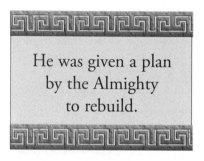

He was given a plan by the Almighty to rebuild.

Many of us are in the same boat as the people of Israel: we are inhabitants in a world that continues to offer temptations that can lead us into sin, and we are desperately trying to build walls around us to keep them away. But we all know that we get tired and fatigued and our prayer life, meditation time and Bible time isn't what it should be. It is in those times that we let our guard down.

Nehemiah 4:15-23 teaches us that we should always be equipped for an enemy advance. Pick up your Bible and read verses 16-18: "*And it came from that day on that half of my servants carried on the work while half of hem held the spears, the shields, the bows, and the breastplates, and the captain were behind the whole house of Judah. Those who were rebuilding the wall and those who carried burdens took their load with one hand doing the work and the other holding a weapon. As for the builders, each wore his sword girded at his side, as he built, while the trumpeter stood near me.*"

By being on the lookout for evil, the wall was rebuilt in record time.

Take the advice of Nehemiah and keep your spiritual armor on and guard up. That's the only effective way to keep evil-doers from harming you, your family and friends.

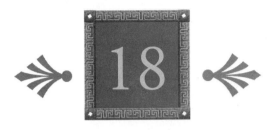

# A spiritual graduation

It was a hot and muggy night in June 1999 as I drove down the nearly vacant highways of Houston. The temperature had been climbing all across the city. To my left was the eight wonder of the world — known in the Space City as the Astrodome. And to my right was a man who could easily be considered a wonder of this world — Harvard's Dr. Cornel West (he's since moved to Princeton).

It was such a sight to see. Dr. Cornel West was still wearing his trademark black three-piece suit, huge afro blowing in the winds as a result of the top of my Mazda Miata being let down. Hey, it was 99 degrees at 4 a.m. We couldn't help it!

As my Alpha Phi Alpha frat brother enjoyed the sweet jazz coming from the speakers in the seat, my soul was busy; troubled by the dilemma I was facing. For you see, I had walked away from the Catholic Church after 25 years. My church attendance was spotty at best. I was perplexed because my soul had been anchoring for a change of scenery. As a man then in his mid-20's, I was looking for a significant level of relevance in my spiritual life and the Catholic Church, though wondrous to me for so many years, was no longer the answer. In essence, I was dying a slow death because my spirit was no longer being fed.

I reached down to throttle the radio down to ask Dr. West, a noted theologian, what had been bothering me for months. After telling him about a church in Dallas that I was interested in attending — I loved the pastor's commitment to social equality and justice — I was perplexed because I had been such a died in the wool Catholic.

All too often our spirits are no longer comfortable in the same place

"Ah," he said in his trademark tone, stroking his beard as he contemplated my dilemma. "Brother Martin, it's a rather common problem. You see, when I'm in a contemplative mood, I will attend a Catholic Church. There''s something about the quietness of it that allows me to think and reflect on my issues. When I need to have my butt whipped, I will attend my old-fashioned black Baptist Church because of the strong delivery of the Word. Now, my wife is Ethiopian, and I don't know what they are saying, chanting and beating on the drums, but the rhythmic sounds they make is such a strong presence in me that it has a spiritual effect."

"Dang," I thought. "This brother's good." I thanked him for that small yet wonderful explanation because it cleared up so many of the misconceptions that were going through my mind.

The conversation is even as clear to me today as it was six years ago because it clearly highlighted a problem so many of us face. After so many years of attending one church, we often assume that we are meant to be born, baptized, married and buried in the same place.

But all too often our spirits are no longer comfortable in the same place.

We begin to get restless. No longer do we think about the message being taught but instead, wonder what we will fix for dinner, what movie we will catch that night or what the score is in the football game of our favorite team.

That mental escapism is what caused me to question my presence in the Catholic Church. I found myself reciting the Apostle's Creed and the other mantras without any thought to what I was saying. I was basically "The Walking (Spiritually) Dead."

As believers in the body of Christ, we are to constantly be challenged and fed by the Word of God. Yet when it seems that we are no longer receiving that, far too many of us fall into a hole and never choose to come out of it.

God has impressed upon me that what we have to do is graduate from one Christian experience to another.

When I moved from Dallas to Houston, I left my home church and joined another in Houston. Although I loved Friendship-West Baptist Church, God led me to Brookhollow Baptist Church. I stayed there two years before returning to Dallas, yet my spirit wasn''t comfortable in FWBC once I moved back. The same pastor was there; most of the same people were there, yet I felt out of place. I thought it was because I had left and needed some time to adjust, but God made it clear that I was no longer being fed there. This did not mean that the pastor wasn't doing his job; he was. But God needed — no, He required — me to go elsewhere because what He had for me to do made it necessary. I had to forego my will and what I thought was right and completely let go and say, "God, wherever you think I need to go is where I will go." I had basically graduated from one spiritual level to another. In layman's terms, I had been granted my papers from high school and now it was time for me to go to college. And when I finished my B.S., it was time for me to go after my master's.

It finally dawned on me that that was what Dr. West was ministering to me about that night in 1995. We have to submit ourselves to the will of God and go where He wants us to go. Isn't it amazing that we get that itchy feeling about a job and begin to look for another, yet we don't have the same attitude about our Christian experience?

Many of you may be sitting in a place where you have grown comfortable and cozy in the Word. No longer are you reading with zest or being challenged by the Word. No longer are you reading and studying and listening to tapes and asking questions. It could very well mean that you have graduated from the place you are in and God needs to plant you somewhere else to accomplish His goals.

# Listening to the Spirit Within

I know it's difficult to leave a place where you and your family have grown comfortable. I feel you when you say that your leaving may create a void or may give the impression that you had a falling out with a pastor. It's important for you to convey to those around you the true nature for your leaving and why you need to continue onward to your spiritual growth.

I loved listening to Pastor Haynes. He was a young, dynamic man, and personally, we were fraternity brothers of Alpha Phi Alpha. But I had to listen to God tell me, "I need you to make this move because what I have in store for you requires it." Remember, in John 21 Jesus told John to take care of his sheep and to watch over them. Jesus wanted them to be continuously fed the Word of God so they could have the sustenance to live and thrive. Be mindful of that Word.

Continue to pray and meditate on being in a place where you are constantly being fed and taught. And if it feels like you are going over the same lessons over and over, don't fret and begin to badmouth the pastor and the deacons.

That could simply be God's way of saying that you have graduated, and it's time to elevate yourself to the next spiritual level.

# Willing to bow down and surrender

*Text focus: Mark 1:40-42*

\*\*\*

One of the hardest things for Christians — and even those who have not professed that Jesus is Lord — is to bring their cares and concerns to the altar, bow down and ask God for his guidance and healing.

So many of us are more concerned with what the person next to us will think if they see us slip out of the aisle and walk to the altar for prayer, rather than casting our cares onto a God who can handle any and everything we have to offer.

When this passage of Mark is preached or discussed, the emphasis is normally on Jesus' willingness to heal the man with leprosy, a disease that caused people in biblical days to react much in the same way we do today to someone who has AIDS.

Yet as I was studying this passage, God put it upon my heart to read it a bit differently. As opposed to giving Jesus all the glory — even though he richly deserves it — God said, "Roland, the emphasis should be on the man with leprosy because he was willing to approach my son, bow down and humbly ask for a blessing." I had to go back and re-read the passage and it was so clear: the man with leprosy came to Jesus and begged him on his knees. The man with leprosy didn't sit on his living room couch and hope he would be cured of such a debilitating illness; he didn't ask a friend to pray for him to be healed; he got up, despite the pain of leprosy, approached Jesus, fell on his knees and begged, "If you are willing…"

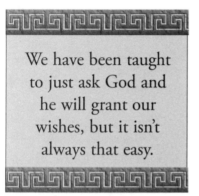

We have been taught to just ask God and he will grant our wishes, but it isn't always that easy.

Use your sanctified imagination for a bit. The man with leprosy probably visited doctors all around his home yet got no good news. People with leprosy were discarded and treated with utter contempt. Realizing he had no other choice and that he had hit rock bottom, I'm sure the man said, "I keep hearing about this man who can heal. I might as well try and see what he can do."

When is the last time you did that? When was the last time you forgot about your husband, wife, family, friends, coworkers or anyone else and slipped out of that aisle in church, or delayed your sleep to fall on your knees to cry out to

God, "If you are willing…"

I know we have been taught to just ask God and he will grant our wishes, but it isn't always that easy. Sometimes we have to make the extra effort in order to receive God''s blessings.

I think back to 1999 when I was mired in a major financial crisis. I had just moved to Houston to join my then-wife. Choosing my marriage over career, I gave up 60% of my income to do so. Due to breaking leases and things like that, it cost me a pretty penny to make the move. All was well until one month after my move; my wife decided that she no longer wanted to be married. Here I was: moving for the second time in two months, desperately trying to find financial resources that prior to my move was easy to tap into.

Sitting at my desk at the *Houston Defender*, I poured over my budget and checkbook. Trust me, it didn't look good at all. "Lord, I have not seen numbers like this since college," I said. I cried out, "Lord, now, I'm not mad at you, but I'm pretty ticked off now. I've done all you said to do, I've followed you, I've listened to you, yet I'm sitting here, broke, marriage ending and I don't know where to turn. So, I'm tired of this. You are going to have to find me some money to handle this situation."

With that, I rubbed my hands together with some blessed oil, put one hand on my checkbook and another on my budget and commenced to fervently pray.

The next day I told the story to the publisher of the paper, Sonny Messiah-Jiles. Listening intently, she asked me to close the door.

"Roland, I''ve been meaning to tell you this for the last two months, but I've been so busy," she said. "Because you are taking photos, writing and editing stories, you are saving us a lot of money. So I''m going to add $5,000 to your salary. I've been meaning to tell you, but I guess God wanted you to ask first."

I looked up and said, "Dang, God, that was quick!"

The focus of this story isn't that fervently praying to God will result in a financial windfall. Instead, it's about being obedient to His word and choosing to fall on your knees and ask Him to provide a blessing if He is willing. Despite my anger and frustration, God didn't owe me a thing. But He chose to bless me. Yet without asking, it's likely the blessing would not have been released. I had to be broken down completely before I would say such a prayer.

And that is what God wants so many of us to. Much like the man with leprosy, He wants us to submit ourselves to His will, get on bended knee and cry out to Him to heal us from our present predicament.

There's no sense in carrying around the pain and anxiety that accompanies your problem. Cast your worries on God, listen to His directions and see Him move on your behalf.

# 'Down' can get you up on unconditional love

*First published in the Dallas Weekly on Dec. 22, 1998*

\*\*\*

If you venture out to the malls or any retail store during this Christmas season, there is little doubt you will encounter a horde of people ripping and running to buy that perfect gift for that special loved one.

The size of the gift — or its price tag — is sometimes based on our love for someone else, which often leads us to spending an inordinate amount of money just to bring a smile to that person's face.

But all too often we forget what the real reason for Christmas is — our undying faith and celebration of the birth of Jesus Christ, and as a part of that celebration the importance of His unconditional love for us.

Over the past couple of weeks I have been reading the bestseller, *Conversations with God*, a rich and powerful expression of God's divine plan for all of us. In the first of the three-book series, writer Neal Donald Walsch writes about what God told him about unconditional love and its importance in our lives. We all have our own definitions of love, but unconditional love is something that often eludes us.

I have been grappling with trying to understand the true meaning of unconditional love. That is, until God led me to see Maya Angelou's *Down in the Delta*.

# 'Down' can get you up on unconditional love

In *Delta*, Earl (Al Freeman Jr.) is an elderly man living in Mississippi who has taken in his deceased brother's daughter and her two children so she can get her life together. Although Loretta (Alfre Woodard) is the central focus of this movie, it wasn't the reaffirmation of life for her that caught my attention. Instead, it was Earl'''s undying love for his wife, Aunt Annie (Esther Rolle).

You see, Aunt Annie and Earl have been married for a number of years; raising a loving son, Will (Wesley Snipes); maintaining a restaurant, and loving one another. But Annie can no longer do for herself because Alzheimer's has taken her mind and her ability to live without assistance.

> Unconditional love affords us the opportunity to see what that person needs and try to satisfy their request.

Yet despite Annie behaving somewhat like a child — unable to remember to flush the toilet, much less her husband's name — Earl doesn't stop loving his Annie. When she begins to babble, Earl holds her hand, telling her everything will be okay. When Annie gets scared Earl is there to reassure her that everything will be just fine. When Will doesn't want to come home for Annie's birthday because his mother doesn't even remember him, Earl tells Will that it's important that he celebrate his mother's birthday. Home, he says, is just that — home.

As the story unfolded, it became increasingly evident how important Earl's love for Annie was. Sure, he could have placed here in a nursing home for someone else to care for her, but he didn't. At one point Loretta makes that suggestion, only to have Earl lightly admonish her by saying, "She needs home." Earl clearly became selfless by putting the needs of his wife before his own self-centered concerns.

It is that unconditional love Earl had for Annie that many of us must have for our wives, husbands, friends and family. Far too often we get focused on our jobs, the latest gadgets, golf, traveling, and what others think of us that we forget we should be feeling for one another. We also hold onto grudges, harsh words and other actions spoken against us by our spouses and others. Although we can forgive co-workers for saying some un-Godly things toward us, we don't seem to have the same forgiveness and compassion for the person we sleep next to.

It is understandable that many of us are selfish in wanting our needs to be met. But we often forget there is someone else in our life that is looking for that same thing. Unconditional love affords us the opportunity to see what that person needs and try to satisfy their request.

Unconditional love also extends beyond the boundaries of marriage; it is also imperative in our family life. We may have family members who are on drugs or in jail, but God tells us that they are family and they, too, deserve our unconditional love and prayers.

So during this Christmas season, after you've opened your gifts, had a wonderful dinner and thanked God for your blessings, take the time to see *Down in the Delta*, and see the Unconditional love that is portrayed throughout the film. And maybe instead of giving someone an expensive gift or a new toy, maybe you ought to give them the one thing God grants to us every day: unconditional love.

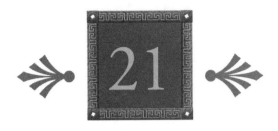

# A worthy praise

**Text focus: Isaiah 12**
***

It's amazing how we are so quick to say, "Praise the Lord" when we have purchased a new car or house or gotten a raise, yet even the simplest things in life don't make us just shout and say, "Lord, you are so good and worthy of praise."

As I write this essay I am sitting on the balcony of the largest cruise ship in the world, the Royal Caribbean Explorer. There is a brisk breeze that feels so wonderful. The waves are crashing against the ship and the skies are so clear that the stars seem as if they are perpetually winking at me. As I look out across the water there comes a point when the sky and water seem to come together — one indistinguishable from the other.

In many respects that could describe our opportunities to praise. We have taken on such a bland position about praise that we have become indifferent. But Isaiah 12 clearly shows us that we shouldn't do that — not even when we are dead tired and don't feel like saying a word.

When we are in such a dour position when it comes to praise, remember Isaiah 12:1 where it says that God will comfort us, regardless of the situation. That's enough to shout all day! We have been assaulted with bad news, our finances are in shambles and our children are driving us absolutely bananas, yet here is a God that comforts us.

When faced with such a thing we should also take on an air of confidence because the comfort of God means that he is present, and in the presence of God, we, as it says in Isaiah 12:3, should not be afraid.

We are told to trust in the Lord because He is my strength and my salvation and my song. When I first read that in the NIV translation, I was thrown off by "song." In essence, what that means is in a time of trouble I can cry out his name or call on him in song. See, I don't need to remember him only when singing "We Fall Down" or "Amazing Grace." Just His name alone represents more of a comfort than any lyrics in a song. Just His name reveals a feeling that is more moving than any Yolanda Adams song. God is God, and His name is worthy to be praised.

> Always remember that God does not have to be enclosed in a box on God does not have to be enclosed in a box on Sunday or Wednesday.

And lastly, when we have remembered that God is a comforting God, than we have nothing to fear in His presence. We have a responsibility to tell the story.

How many of you have heard Paul Harvey's show? I love it, especially when he says in his distinctive voice, "Now the rest of the story." Isaiah 12:4-6 represents the rest of the story when it comes to praise. He has comforted us, hasn't abandoned us, and has provided a safe haven from fear and He has given us strength. After all of that we have nothing left to do but praise Him and tell someone else how good He has been. We are told in a very specific way what to do:

1. Give thanks to the Lord.
2. Call on His name.
3. Tell everybody what He has done.
4. Proclaim the exalted God.
5. Shout and sing for joy regarding His greatness.

# A worthy praise

Always remember that God does not have to be enclosed in a box on Sunday or Wednesday.

We don't have to restrict the calling of His name when we have acquired a material blessing. Our praise for Him should be continuous; a day should never go by where we don't offer Him the praise for everything that we have.

# Showing gratitude for God's blessings

**Text focus: Numbers 11**

\*\*\*

If there was one year that was one of the most difficult I have ever faced, 2000 would be it.

In June of 1999, I was divorced, and six months later, I met the woman that God told me that I would marry. The last thing I wanted to do was take another walk down the aisle — the pain was too much after six years of marriage — but the Lord said, "You can do whatever you want to do. But this is the woman that I have set aside for you."

End of conversation.

What concerned me wasn't just getting married again, it was also the financial problems I was enduring. I had lots of debt from the marriage, and on top of that, God told me to move back to Dallas from Houston and to use all of my 401K savings to buy a house. I didn't have a job, and the Lord was telling me that I will buy a home because all that He had for me business-wise required me to return to Dallas. On top of that, God ordered me to leave everything from the marriage. I could have walked away with at least $100,000, but he said, "No. I forbid it."

I did, and trust me, the problems began immediately. The bills began to pile up and in some months, I only brought home $400. Here I was in a relationship with a woman who God said would be my wife and I couldn't even pay the phone bill some months. This wasn't the kind of impression I wanted to give. But all God kept telling me was, "I will supply your needs."

This went on for about 15 months. I almost came close to losing my home to foreclosure three times, but in each case, I would get a call to write a story and that would pay the mortgage.

The lease on my SUV was up, and I couldn't afford to keep it. I held on to it, forcing the company to pick it up. Hey, a brother's gotta do what a brother's gotta do. I began to use my future's wife SUV, but then her transmission went out. One day, I got a check in the mail and had to deposit it in the bank. But the truck was in the shop for two weeks, and I couldn't find a friend to take me to the bank.

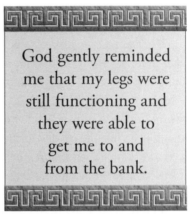

God gently reminded me that my legs were still functioning and they were able to get me to and from the bank.

Desperately needing the money so I could buy groceries, I was left with one choice: walk to the bank.

This was one painful walk. It may have been fall in Dallas, but it was still hot. And on top of that, the bank was a 20-mile round-trip hike! Getting there was no problem; coming back was the hard part. By the time I got home — several hours later — my legs were in intense pain, and I was one unhappy camper.

It was at this point that I threw up my hands and said God, "I just can't take it anymore. I'm broke. I don't have a car. What is going on?"

Then I heard the spirit say, "Do your legs work?"

I replied, "Yes."

"Well," God said, "Didn't I tell you I will supply your needs?"

Here, I was upset and angry about not having any transportation, yet God gently reminded me that my legs were still functioning and they were able to get me to and from the bank.

This story came to mind as I read Numbers 11. The Israelites were led out of bondage in Egypt, and God was hovering over them, protecting them from harm and providing their every need. Stuck in the desert with no food, the Lord provided manna for them to live off of. Numbers 11:7-9 says, "*Manna was a seed-like substance with a shiny appearance like resin. The people went around collecting it and ground it between stones or pounded it fine in a mortar. Then they boiled it in a pot and shaped it into cakes. It tasted like a delicacy cooked in olive oil. When the dew fell on the camp at night, the manna was right there with it.*"

Here was a group of people who didn''t have to lift a finger to eat. All they had to do was go to sleep, wake up and the manna was right there for them. But like many of us today who are ungrateful for all that God provides, the Israelites began to whine, saying they could have stayed in Egypt and had their pick of fish, fruit and other delicacies. Of course, they didn't say a word about being in bondage and tormented by pharaoh. All they could remember were the good ol' days. Sure, the manna didn''t taste as good as the fish, but it sure was better than being beaten and worked to death!

Tired of their groaning, God decide to fix them. He told Moses that He would provide them with so much meat that it would be coming out of their nostrils. And true to his word, that happened. The quail came down so hard in a fierce wind that it stacked up three feet high. Even the slowest moving person was able to get, according to Eugene Petersen's *The Message* biblical translation, at least 60 bushels.

They all had a huge feast, but they couldn't enjoy it for long. Tired of their ungrateful attitude, God dropped a terrible plague on them and "*there they buried the people who craved meat.*" (11:34).

God may not choose to place a plague on your for showing ingratitude, but rest assured that the Lord isn't pleased when we are blessed with health, wealth, prosperity and abundance, and all we do is complain about is this or that. God loves us unconditionally, yet, when we are disobedient, He will punish us for our transgressions.

Those 15 months of financial uncertainty truly taught me what it means to have wants and needs. While I saw the vehicle as a need, it really wasn't. I didn't have a job that required me to get in the car. I was a writer! I could do my job right from my home office. God knew that, but I had to go through the experience to understand what is truly a want and need.

That's why, today, I'm not concerned about the really insignificant stuff in life. Materials possessions such as cars, houses, jewelry, gadgets and other "stuff" really mean nothing to me. I really don't care about going out and running around with a bunch of folks who live in a shallow world. I really and truly sit back and thank God for the most basics of life — my health, a loving and adoring wife and a roof over my head.

Sure, I have dreams and aspirations and want to take exotic vacations and stuff like that. But I refuse to complain about what I already have, and I don't allow those around me to do that.

If you have a car that rides well and is meeting your needs, don't constantly talk about how you wish you were driving this and that. Don't spend unnecessary time talking about what your husband and wife isn't doing compared to a friend. Be honest: you don't know what's going in his or her household. Focus on the good they do; and as for the not so good, pray for them, intercede for them and gently show them how they could improve, but also how YOU can do better!

We all must assume a more grateful role for all that God has blessed us with. We must, as Yolanda Adams says in her song, "Thank You," "take advantage of this chance and say thank you." There have been so many days when I looked at my wife and all that we have been through and tears nearly come to my eyes and all I can say is "thank you." I am left with no choice but to continue to praise God and say, "Thank you, thank you, thank you."

I am confident that when we thank the Lord for ALL that He has provided for us-big or small-and allow our worship to be based on adoration and not a need to ask for stuff, then the Lord will truly open the doors and pour out a bountiful blessing that will be more than we can handle.

# 23

# Prepare yourself for the journey

*Text focus: 1 Kings 19:3-9*

***

When I worked as managing editor of The *Dallas Weekly*, one of the responsibilities of my assistant, Manaqua, was to remind me to eat. At the time, I was also news director/morning anchor at a local radio station, and when I got off of work at 9 a.m., I would head straight to the paper.

On the way there, I would be on the phone with a variety of people, trying to get a handle on what was in the paper, status of stories, photos and other useful information. Only later, would I glance at the clock and realize that I had been up for 12 hours, working hard, and hadn't stopped for a meal. My body would be tired and a headache would arrive, and I would struggle to get out of the door to grab something — anything — to keep going for a few more hours.

After a few weeks, Manaqua solved this dilemma. Every day around noon, she would stop me dead in my tracks and ask if I had eaten. The response would often be "no" and I would just keep on working or say I'll get something later. She would then throw me a "yea, right" look, march over, stick her hand out and make me give her some money for food. If she was returning from lunch she would cal land ask the receptionist if I had eaten. If the answer was no, I could expect her to come back with lunch.

Manaqua realized that I was so engrossed in my work that food was the last thing on my mind. But she understood that I couldn't continue that way. Food provided the fuel for me to keep driving the paper to achieve excellence.

My former assistant came to mind as I read Elijah's dilemma in 1 Kings 19.

After exerting so much work in chewing up the prophets of Baal, Elijah was tired. His life became even crazier when Ahab's wife, Jezebel, sent a messenger to tell Elijah that she would do to him what he did to Baal's prophets-completely destroy them.

God has heard your cries, can feel your pain and doesn't like you frustrated.

He didn't waste any time and just took off.

After a day in the desert, Elijah had had enough and just threw up his hands and said, *"I have had enough"* (v4).

For all of these years he had been fighting with Ahab, Jezebel, the prophets and everyone else. The man was fed by ravens, told a woman who was at her wits end to feed him some bread and oil when she had none, and performed miracle after miracle. You would think he would have received some gratitude, but Elijah was engaged in some serious warfare. Here was a man coming off his greatest victory but was now scared and tired.

Have you been where Elijah was? Have you been running and running, doing what the Lord has told you, but it appears as if nothing has changed? God is telling me that there is a wife reading this who has been praying and praying for her husband to find the Lord and lead his family, yet he seems further and further away from the altar. There is a husband who is keeping the family together while his wife is overwhelmed by her job. He is nurturing the kids and trying to keep the spark going between him and his wife, yet her inattentiveness and lack of intimacy is quashing that dim light. There is a pastor or ministry leader who has given and given, only to have to deal with an unappreciative congregation. There is an entrepreneur who is shedding tears of frustration because God has told you to launch that business, but you are hitting the brick wall as the company fights just to keep the doors open.

As a result, your bills are late, vendors want to be paid and you seem to be swimming upstream.

Please understand. God has heard your cries, can feel your pain and doesn't like you frustrated. But the Lord wants you to know that the pain you are experiencing is a short-term sacrifice for this journey you are on.

God knows that you can't handle all of this alone. The moment where you feel like you can't take it anymore is the point where the Lord says, "I got it."

Elijah had reached that point and that's when God sent an angel to provide him with a cake and a jar of water (v6). The angel then woke him up again so he could eat because *"the journey is too much for you"* (v7).

Yet this time wasn't just about eating. Elijah also took the time to rest.

When we are planning or driving a great distance, we all make the effort to get lots of rest and eat because we need all of our strength so we can be fresh and alert. God needed a well-rested Elijah to be rested and well fed because his task wasn't complete. Read the rest of 1 Kings. Elijah went on to anoint Elisha as his successor; he was to confront Ahab again; and then ascended to heaven.

The Lord is trying to tell you the same thing. You are tired and frustrated, but God wants to revive, refresh and renew your spirit.

1. **He will give you rest**. Don't think that you are in this fight alone. The Lord wants you to rest in His bosom and be comforted by His presence. Psalm 23 says, *"He makes me lie down in green pastures, he leads me beside quiet waters. He restores my soul."* God wants you to settle down and allow Him to speak to your spirit. Your prayer and meditation time is crucial to getting rid of the anxiety and quieting your spirit. When you begin to feel the comforting presence of the Holy Spirit, then you can count on your situation being resolved.

2. **He will feed you a plentiful meal**. When your spirit is under assault you need to be fortified, and that only happens through the word of God. You can't expect to battle spiritual matters with your husband, wife, children, boss or congregation and not be in the word of God.

Scripture is our sustenance. When we hunger for direction and guidance, we can only get that through reading and studying of the word of God. We may hear a sermon on TV or radio or listen to the advice and counsel of a friend, but our spirit will only be nourished when we feast on God's word.

Whatever journey God has for you on isn't easy. You will be faced with all kinds of difficulties and roadblocks, but don't fear and give up. God is ready to walk, ride or run in front, behind and over you wherever you are going.

# Children can
# be a witness, too

*Text focus: Matthew 9:10-13*

\*\*\*

The email was an urgent appeal for money. A father who had lost a source of income was forced to pull his three children out of Christian schools and put them in public schools.

All had been well for a couple of weeks, but then his oldest daughter came to him one night in tears. She was devastated because her new school was 180 degrees different from the Christian school she attended. Students cussed, were disrespectful to teachers and engaged in conduct that was foreign to her.

Her father was just crushed. He wanted to rescue his daughter but his wallet couldn't comply. And that's when he sent an urgent email to friends and family seeking funds from friends to help put his daughter back in a Christian school.

When the email arrived, I had two initial thoughts. First, I truly felt for the child's father because he wanted the best for his child. He wanted her to be in an environment that challenged her, comforted her and allowed her to grow. Yet I also felt for the other students who didn't have a chance to go to school in the safe confines of a Christian school. Their parents didn't have the discretionary income; public school was their only alternative. I know the feeling. That was the only choice my parents could make in order for their five children to get educated.

Yet as I began to ponder the situation, God began to speak to my spirit and raise a few other points.

We live in a world where sin is in abundance. Topless bars, adult stores, alcohol, drugs and other societal ills are all around us. We can't turn on the television without having to grab the remote if our children walk into the room.

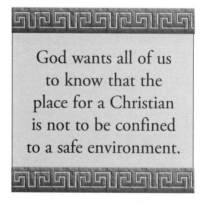

**God wants all of us to know that the place for a Christian is not to be confined to a safe environment.**

It would be easy to stay indoors and only venture out to shop, work and go to church.

God wants all of us to know that the place for a Christian is not to be confined to a safe environment. Somehow we need to allow our light to shine in the midst of darkness.

When the Pharisees heard that Jesus was eating with a variety of sinners they were stunned. But Jesus told them that it is the sick that need a doctor.

What we should be doing is encouraging our children to not accept this kind of behavior as the thing that other teenagers do. Instead of sheltering them, we should be building up their faith and teaching them how to wear their spiritual armor. I believe that if we had more teenagers who represent the Lord at school, we would see a remarkable transformation. Stop complaining about there being no prayer in school. Let's teach this generation the importance of having a God-like attitude and encourage them to cultivate other students. Jesus didn't say that only adults could witness and disciple. Anyone who professes that Jesus Christ is Lord is called to take up the cross.

I can't say for sure that Christian students allowing their spirits to take root and spread to the classroom will transform every public school. But I am confident that if they are willing to represent God at all times, his presence will envelope any place they inhabit, thus touching any and everyone who comes near.

# A healing presence

*Text focus: Acts 5:12-16*
***

I love guys like Henderson Lee.

Henderson is a member of my church in Houston — Brookhollow Baptist Church, also known as The Church Without Walls.

There hasn't been a Sunday when I have seen Henderson before or after church and his presence didn't light up the place. He is always smiling and ready to embrace anyone he comes into contact with. You may be feeling down, but being in the presence of Henderson will undoubtedly raise your spirits.

Is there a Henderson Lee in your life? Is there a family member, friend or co-worker who causes you to feel good after you've seen them? Do you desperately need a person like that surrounding you at all times?

In many ways these people help us just like Peter and the apostles did in Acts 5.

These guys were on a roll. They *"performed many miracles, signs and wonders among the people"* (v12).

It seems that when they healed one group, another just as large followed. Their exploits became so great that the people were amazed by their healing power and "people brought the sick into the streets and laid them on beds and mats so that at least Peter's shadow might fall on some of them as he passed by."

# A healing presence

Later it is recorded that "all of them were healed."

Now is that power or what?! You know the Holy Spirit has showed up and showed out when your passing shadow is able to heal people!

We should all take that to heart because we don't realize how our attitude can mean the world to someone. All too often we underestimate the power of a smile or a hello. My wife gets a kick out of me walking through an office and speaking to secretaries and janitors the same way I would a CEO or a member of Congress. An individual title is irrelevant to me. What I care most about is treating each person like a human being.

> You know the Holy Spirit has showed up and showed out when your passing shadow is able to heal people!

Does this mean that Peter's positive attitude healed the sick? No, it was the anointing on Peter from God that resulted in his healing power. Yet what we must realize is that our own attitudes and actions can have a similar effect on the emotional needs of those around us.

Now, if a positive attitude can have a healing presence, a negative demeanor can kill a good time. How many times have you found yourself having a good time at lunch, only to have a mad and negative co-worker plop down? What was a fun time has now turned sour because of their mere presence. Party pooper!

I known we are not taught to hate people, but I HATE NEGATIVE PEOPLE! If you are a perpetual negative person, don't even come near me. No, really. Please move on to the next person. Better yet, go home. I don't want you spoiling it for anyone else. And don't come near my wife, parents, brother, sisters or my nieces or nephews. Negativity is one of the worst human traits in the world.

Your mere appearance or presence may heal someone of an affliction. I do believe that when someone else sees the God in you, they will be comforted by whatever troubles them. Your presence can have a healing effect on their situation.

Be sure to make it your mission that as you pass through this life on your way to heaven, your shadow can be a healing presence for others.

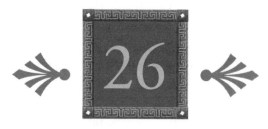

# Fight for your healing

*Text focus: Mark 2:2-5; 5:24(b)-34*

\*\*\*

When I joined Brookhollow Baptist Church/The Church Without Walls in 1999, some of my friends thought I was crazy to drive more than one-hour roundtrip just to attend the church.

There were many churches in close proximity to where I lived — right across from Houston's Astrodome — but I never had a sense that God wanted me to join those fine churches.

In fact, in December 1998, God clearly told me to make my way to Brookhollow.

At that time I was living in Dallas and preparing to move to Houston. On one Monday, the Lord kept telling me to listen to one of several tapes by the Rev. Ralph Douglas West. I picked up the tapes because Pastor West had often visited my church in Dallas, Friendship-West Baptist Church, and I was so moved by them that I bought them.

All week I listened to the tapes. It was certainly a weird experience because I had owned them for months, and had never really listened to them again after buying them.

By the time Friday arrived, I was on my way to Houston to see my first wife. All God kept telling me was to visit The Church Without Walls.

That Saturday I told Deborah that I wanted to visit Brookhollow. She really didn't say much so I figured it was no problem. I awoke Sunday morning and reminded her of the church service, and she got upset.

"What's wrong with my church?"

"Nothing," I said. "I've simply been wanting to visit Brookhollow all week."

I could tell that she was ticked off, but it really didn't matter. God was telling me where to go and I wasn't going to be disobedient.

We arrived at the church and one of the first folks we ran into was my cousin, Antoinette Latham, and her mom, my Aunt Pam. It was certainly a joy to see friendly faces.

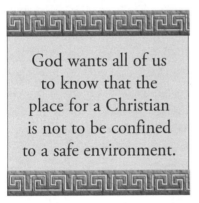

God wants all of us to know that the place for a Christian is not to be confined to a safe environment.

On that Sunday, Pastor West preached a powerful sermon. As we sat in the massive sanctuary, there was an immediate sense of comfort. I knew at that moment I was sitting in the right place.

Even though there were about 1,800 people in that service — the second of three — I made my way to the front to greet Pastor West. We had met briefly during one of his visits in Dallas, and we discussed something we had in common — golf and our membership in Alpha Phi Alpha Fraternity, Inc.

We greeted one another as brothers in Christ (and Alpha), and Pastor West asked about our church attendance. Deborah told him that she had joined another church, and Pastor West said that was a pretty good choice (it was pastored by a friend of his). Then I said, "Well, that was before I moved here."

Boy, she threw me a look that could have frozen a lot of people! When we got into the car she immediately jumped on the comment. "What do you mean 'that was before I moved here?"

I explained to her precisely what I meant; that she joined the church, but during my many visits there I had never felt comfortable in the place. I never felt led or called to that church and didn't think it was going to meet our spiritual needs.

"So what are you going to do? Go to one church and I go to another?"

"No," I said. "I can only go where the Lord is leading me to go."

Well, after I moved two months later, it wasn't long before I moved again — out of our house. She wanted a divorce and that's the way it was going to be.

The disagreement over the church wasn't the reason for the divorce; the marriage had been on the rocks for about two years. But the spiritual gulf that was between the two of us was evident.

I had no idea why the Lord had led me to Brookhollow, but I knew that I had to trust God.

In the ensuing months, what was unclear to me became crystal clear: God knew full well that my marriage was going to end, and he needed me in a place where I was going to be taught an uncompromising word, and where I could be sustained through the separation, and healed through the divorce.

Even though I lived miles and miles away, there was no way that I could allow any distance or barriers such as construction or the need to fill up my tank two to three times a week as a reason for me not attending Brookhollow.

I've heard many people say, "I just want to go to a church that is near my home." Instead of allowing God to lead them to a place where they can be fed spiritually, they take the easy way out.

Now I don't know about you, but I am willing to face down any obstacle to get to a place where God wants to restore and revive me!

My willingness to overlook obstacles isn't new. In fact, all I did was do exactly what two of God's chosen people in the Bible did.

Mark 2 tells us about a paralytic who refused to stay in his present condition and that he would do anything to be healed by Jesus.

When the Son of God arrived in Capernaum, the crowds were unbelievably large. Imagine a biblical e-mail blast being sent out across the region; folks coming from near and far just to experience a miracle with Jesus.

The paralytic was at a severe disadvantage. He couldn't walk, which meant he would be run over and potentially crushed by the crowd. So four men carried him to Jesus. But the crowds were still too much for them. These days, if a person in a wheelchair comes our way, we often clear the path and allow them to go ahead of us. Yet this crowd was jockeying for position so much that the paralytic's needs came after their own.

Luckily, these four men did not allow these obstacles to get in their way. Scripture says that "they made an opening in the roof above Jesus and, after digging through it, lowered the mat the paralyzed man was lying on. When Jesus saw their faith, he said to the paralytic, "Son, your sins are forgiven."

Jesus later rewarded another person who was willing to keep fighting in order to be blessed.

Mark 5 tells us of the woman with the blood problem. For 12 years she had been afflicted. Despite visiting doctor after doctor and spending a ton of money, it was all to no avail. This was a woman who was sick and tired of being sick and tired. She wanted to be healed and would do everything she could in her power to get to Jesus during his visit to the region of the Gerasenes.

In a message entitled, "Fighting Your Way Through Adversity: Making Your Way Through the Crowd," Pastor West said this woman was remarkable because:

1. She didn't allow her sickness to hinder her.
2. She established her goal and set out to seek the answer.
3. She exhausted every human possibility and realized only He could be her rescuer.
4. She never took her eyes off her subject — Jesus.
5. She also didn't allow the crowd's size to thwart her mission.

When Jesus stopped to inquire who touched his cloak, she dropped to her knees, begging forgiveness. But Jesus wasn't mad. He acknowledged that she took a great risk to fight through the crowds to get her healing, and told her, "Daughter, your faith has healed you."

What we all must understand is that it's easy to live a life of convenience.

When faced with challenges, we can do one or two things: face them head on or cower away.

Looking back at my decision to fight the distractions, not worry about eating up gas in my car, and be obedient to my attendance at Brookhollow, I have been tremendously blessed by the experience.

The aftermath of the divorce was truly painful, but God had already dealt with that thing. While my flesh was in pain, my spirit was being cleansed and restored. The Lord rewarded by faith in making my way to 5725 Queenstown Blvd. Had I decided to go somewhere else, I may not have been blessed the way I was at The Church Without Walls.

That blessing was derived from the teaching and preaching Pastor West, the fellowship of its faithful and God-led members, but it is also the place where I met the woman who is now my wife, the Rev. Jacquie Hood Martin.

It certainly was not my intention to be involved in a relationship, especially five months after the divorce was final! But when I met her at the end of November 1999, the Lord told me don't even bother dating any other woman — this is the woman that I have set aside for you.

We should all remember that God sometimes want to see how far we are willing to go in order to serve Him. The woman with the blood problem was healed because she believed Jesus was the Son of God, as well as her willingness to not be dissuaded by the obstacles in front of her.

What today is keeping you from knowing Jesus? What is preventing you from living in God's will? If you are broken and in search of a healing, maybe the Lord wants to see your commitment to seeking Him before he answers your prayers.

If you are too despondent, fine. Find some friends who are willing to bring you to the cross just like the four men who carried the paralytic.

Become a fighter who is willing to do what is necessary to live a life of *"peace and be freed from your suffering"* (Mark 5:34, NIV).

# A test
# of faith

*Text focus: Romans 12:2*

***

The ever-increasing hostile reaction to gay marriage has been a rather difficult proposition for those who consider themselves to be highly educated, fair and honorable.

Many of them take pride in the supremacy of God, yet they are also scared to death to be categorized as someone who would discriminate against another human being based upon their sexual orientation or lifestyle.

It is insightful to watch and listen to my peers discuss the issue. You can even see their college-educated minds whirring and spinning and flipping as they try to figure out some way to not take a side, while at the same time trying to wrestle with the biblical principles they have been taught that homosexuality is a sin and that marriage is between a man and a woman.

If this adequately describes you, let me try to help you out: Just stop. There is no sense in trying to intellectualize something that is clearly laid out and defined in your Bible and mine.

Jesus Christ is the center of my life — and that of my Baptist ordained minister wife — and we have made it our purpose to follow God's will for our lives and try to lead as sinless a life as possible. Do we fail at times? Yes, but that doesn't mean we revel in it. We are honest about it, face it, and then get right back up and fight to stay on the path of righteousness.

Yet what this issue has done, frankly, is force many people to go deep inside of themselves and confront the depth of their faith and how far they are willing to share it and abide by it.

The reality is many gays and lesbians, even those who call themselves Christians, simply don't believe that they are engaging in and living in sin. For them, the grace and mercy and unconditional love of God is far greater than what Leviticus or any other Bible verse says about men being sexually involved with men and women with women. Some say they were born that way while others say all they want to do

We are still held accountable when we sin and are mandated not to do so.

is enjoy the same thing that heterosexuals enjoy: committed love with the blessings of marriage.

Yet my faith simply leads me to a different conclusion. Yes, God offers unconditional love, but we are still held accountable when we sin and are mandated not to do so.

Like it or not, we are a society that has been built on our morals and values. And a significant part of that is based on the idea that the family structure is made up of a man and a woman united in marriage. We have become a great collection of communities, cities and states because of this, which is centered on our faith-based principles.

Gay marriage supporters have effectively used the hypocrisy of church leaders' refusal to preach against rampant divorce while they oppose gay marriage to counter their arguments. But that doesn't mean their lack of resolve on one issue should mean silence on another.

Supporters have also bolstered their arguments by comparing their fight with that of the civil rights movement. They trumpet as supporters of gay marriage and/or civil unions, prominent African Americans such as the Revs. Jesse Jackson and Al Sharpton; Coretta Scott King, and university scholars and theologians, Cornel West and Michael Eric Dyson. I admire and respect them all, but on this issue we will simply agree to disagree. Racism and slavery were just as sinful as homosexuality. No one is greater than the other. It was a matter of Christians taking biblical passages completely out of context in order to satisfy their fleshly desires to oppress blacks.

As a Christian, I am called upon to uphold the word of God and will be judged by the Holy Spirit on whether I did so when given the chance. I can't have a buffet faith: I'll take a little bit of that, some of that, but pass up on that. My faith simply will not allow me to support gay marriage, which runs counter to the beliefs that govern my very existence.

# Broadening the focus of the church

*Text focus: Ephesians 6*
\*\*\*

Adultery. Divorce. Fornication. Domestic violence. Materialism. Absent fathers. Obesity. Greed. Anger.

My dear evangelical friends, please, take your pick. Now that your hackles have been raised over the prospects of homosexuals getting married, maybe you can now tackle with the same level of vigor many of the other "sins" that have led to the moral decay of our nation.

I previously stated my opposition to gay marriage based upon my Christian faith. Yet I refuse to be one of the hypocritical members of the community of faith who rises to protest one issue, while ignoring the others.

It is disingenuous to assign blame to gays and lesbians for bringing about the downfall of marriage in America. That rests completely with heterosexuals and their unwillingness to properly choose partners; failure in receiving pre-marital counseling; and then putting their petty and selfish pleasures above their marriage and family.

About half of the marriages in this country end in divorce, and the faith community are not exempt from these figures. Research from the Barna Research Group shows that born again Christians are more likely to divorce than non-Christians. When gays and lesbians tell me that Jesus never said a word about homosexuality, I remind them that in Matthew 19 he did say that marriage is between a man and woman (do we need to get any clearer than that?). But he also said that God hates divorce, but Moses only granted it "because your hearts were hard."

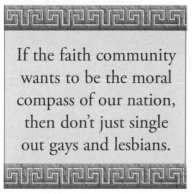

If the faith community wants to be the moral compass of our nation, then don't just single out gays and lesbians.

Maybe ministers across the nation should declare a day of atonement and make the issue of divorce a major topic, instead of just gay marriage.

Many divorces today are a result of adultery. We like to put a nice label on it by saying someone is "having an affair." This is not to say that preachers are not routinely speaking out on adultery, yet the volume seems to be higher on one subject than the other.

The same goes for domestic violence. EndAbuse.org reports that in 2001, more than half a million women were victims of nonfatal domestic violence committed by an "intimate partner."

Again, for my evangelical friends, Ephesians 5 says a man is to love his wife's body as his own, "after all, no one ever hated his own body, but he feeds and cares for it, just as Christ does the church..."

Black pastors in particular have been outspoken in their opposition to gay marriage. The flipside to their moral stand is that they have not fully embraced ministries that are able to deal with the rising HIV/AIDS infection in the black community. White gay men are not the fastest rising group affected by HIV/AIDS. It is black women, and men who sleep with other men, yet they don't consider themselves to be gay, are infecting a significant number.

Absent fathers has reached epic proportions in this country. We know that children are healthier when raised by a mother and a father, yet men are increasingly leaving their families to fend for themselves, and that is not a good thing. In the black community, this is pervasive. As many as 70 percent of black children come into this world out of wedlock. Preachers, are you telling fathers it's time to man up?

Bishop Eddie L. Long, senior pastor of 25,000-member New Birth If the faith community wants to be the moral compass of our nation, then don't just single out gays and lesbians.

Missionary Baptist Church in Atlanta, got so tired of the obesity in his congregation that he begin to do something about it, pushing his members to eat right and workout. We are instructed by scripture to not abuse our temples — the body — and not to gorge on food. So where is the outcry to this burgeoning health hazard?

There is a tremendous amount of good that is derived from our faith community, yet there is so much more that can be done. If the faith community wants to be the moral compass of our nation, then don't just single out gays and lesbians. Put a target on every other member of your congregation and begin to hold them accountable to the same Bible.

# A bold faith

*Text focus: Acts 18:9-10, 25, 28*

\*\*\*

Does anyone know that you are a Christian?

Don't be offended; it really is an important question. I've discovered that Christians are willing to celebrate the power of Jesus Christ, yet when we leave the friendly confines of the church or our concentric circle of holy friends, the fervor for the Holy Spirit vanishes.

How many of you have had conversations on the job, and the one person who is willing to speak openly about the church they attend and the message the pastor preached on the weekend is always seen as the Jesus freak? But amazingly, when co-workers find their marriages breaking up, children on drugs and beset with health problems, they always seek out the Jesus freak for a little grace and mercy.

It even invades our politics. Jimmy Carter and George W. Bush are two of the more devout presidents when it comes to their faith. And boy, have they taken a lot of heat for that!

We witnessed this seemingly uncomfortable position of being a believer by former Democratic presidential candidate Howard Dean. He admitted to not feeling comfortable discussing the impact of Jesus on his life because he said that's how things are done in the eastern portion of the U.S. Folks living in that part of the country see their faith as being a private matter. Yet when he ventured down South, the tables were turned and he chose to speak out more on the issue. Some saw his public pronouncements as a political tool (I was also initially skeptical). But at least he threw caution to the wind and began to share his faith.

We should all be thankful that Paul, Timothy and the other followers of Christ were not as weak and timid with sharing the good news as Christians today. Carrying a big Bible and listening to gospel music is not enough in a world today where temptations are all around us and so many people are suffering from crisis of conscience.

If you are one of those folks who are uncomfortable with sharing the word of God, remember that Jesus called us to do so. That's right. Many of us are willing to quote scripture back and forth and tell others how they should be living their lives, but in The Great Commission (Matthew 28:16-20), the Lord gave us our marching orders to *"go and make disciples of all nations, baptizing them in the name of the Father and of the Son and of the Holy Spirit, and teaching them to obey everything I have commanded you."* Now, how do you suppose we are supposed to share the word of Jesus, which will lead to someone being saved and then baptized, if you never open your mouth?

Look, I understand. It's not an easy thing to do if that's not your thing. Everyone isn't used to speaking and writing like I am. Yet we are all blessed with unique gifts to get our point across and fulfill the mandate of Jesus. We don't need Tony Robbins or any other motivational speaker to get us in the right frame of mind to perform our Godly duties. Listen to that preacher of preachers —Paul — in Acts 18.

1. *"Do not be afraid"* (18:9). Every one of us lives inside a personal cocoon. Others are willing to go outside of it, while many are perfectly happy minding their own business and not upsetting the apple cart. Maybe you are scared of what the other person will say if you begin to speak openly about Jesus. Hey, it could happen! But don't use that as a reason to keep your mouth closed. Many rejected Jesus when He tried to teach the good news. Living in fear does nothing more than give Satan the upper hand. For every person who is not a member of the kingdom of God, that's one person Satan can use for his

purpose; and that is never a good thing. I do offer this word of caution: don't berate people or keep trying to talk to someone who obviously doesn't want to listen to anything about Jesus. Also, if it comes across friends and co-workers who are of another faith, I don't drop pamphlets on their desk or send them Christian-focused emails. Respect their choice just like I want them to respect mine. Yet if the opportunity presents itself and they want to have a dialogue about Jesus, then be willing to share!

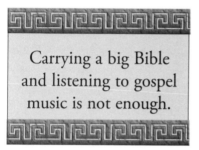

Carrying a big Bible and listening to gospel music is not enough.

2. "*Keep on speaking, do not be silent.* For I am with you…" (v. 9). Remember our good buddy Moses? When God called on him to lead his children out of bondage in Egypt, the Great Emancipator was initially "*Mr. Not Me.*" Exodus 6:30 records that Moses had "*faltering lips*" (*The Message* says he stuttered) and was unsure if Pharaoh would listen to him. So God decided to have Aaron speak for him. If you have difficulty putting the right words together, lean on the understanding of the Lord. There are many times when I want to say the right thing when counseling someone. And when I'm hopping mad and want to curse someone out, I pray Psalm 19:14: "*May the words of my mouth and the meditation of my heart be pleasing in your sight, O Lord, my Rock and my Redeemer*". Begin to make a concerted effort to go into prayer before you begin to share the gospel with others. You may not know what the situation may call for. Only God can reveal to you what needs to be said, if anything at all. Remember, God's got your back.

3. "*He had been instructed in the way of the Lord…and taught about Jesus accurately*" (18:25). There is no way you can proclaim the word of God boldly if you don't know it. I always crack up when I hear a speaker pontificating about a deep and complex issue and they are clearly stumbling and bumbling. That was evidence of not knowing anything about the subject. All that does is leave people more confused than when you started. In order to share the gospel, you have got to read your manual: the Bible. There is no

greater weapon to fight spiritual warfare than scripture. When co-workers or friends visit my office to discuss a moral crisis, they should expect me to speak to them from the wisdom of the Word, and not Dr. Phil or Dr. Laura. I'm not dismissing the words of advice they offer, but my experience has been that there is not a problem in existence that the Bible cannot speak to.

In his book, *Living Faith*, former President Jimmy Carter said he and his wife, Roslyn, had many disagreements in their 30-plus years of marriage. Yet they never had to visit a marriage counselor because they knew who they were in Christ and were mature about their knowledge of God's word.

When the Lord began to impress on me the need to hone my prophetic gift, as well as speaking and teaching, I didn't know where to start. For the first 25 years of my life I was a practicing Catholic, and Bible study was not high on the church's list of priorities. So God commanded me to begin to read three chapters of the Bible each night. By doing this I was able to read and study the word of God, which gave me the confidence to speak authoritatively on a wide range of issues.

Stop calling on your momma, daddy, grandma, prayer partner or pastor when you need to share your faith with someone. Allow God to speak to you through scripture. But that can only happen when YOU pick up the Good Book and begin to read.

There are countless ways in which we can declare our faith and be bold believers. We have at our disposable more gadgets and communication tools than ever before Television, radio, e-mail, two-way pagers, cell phones, books, newspapers and magazines and websites are some of the tools that can be used to share the word of God. These shouldn't be methods that we fear. In fact, I view them not as distractions but great ways to share God's word.

Make a personal decision to not be a silent Christian. Ask the Lord in what ways you should be used for the good of the kingdom and begin to do it today!

# Ordinary people, extraordinary God

*Text focus: Acts 4:13*

\*\*\*

The brainpower of today's generation is the strongest that we have ever existed. When you examine the technological advances that are being discovered each day, everyone should be impressed about how far we've come as a society.

And that even includes the church.

Many of our places of Christian worship are doing work that would be unimaginable years ago. Some churches boast of 50 to 100 ministries that are working with people who have HIV/AIDS; fighting alcoholism and domestic abuse; getting others out of debt; and sending missionaries all over the world to proclaim the gospel of Jesus Christ.

We used to look on with awe when Billy Graham would launch one of his crusades and as many as 50,000 or 100,000 would fill a football or baseball stadium. Today, there are conferences all over the nation that attract tens of thousands of people to hear the word of God.

The rise of the mega-church has been duly noted. Travel to Houston and you can visit Lakewood, a multicultural church that began in a feed store and today is the largest church in the nation, boasting 30,000 members. Travel to Dallas and you can visit The Potter's House, a 26,000-member church led by

Bishop T.D. Jakes. In the Dallas suburb of Plano, Rev. Jack Graham leads Prestonwood Baptist Church. In Atlanta, Bishop Eddie L. Long leads 25,000-member New Birth Missionary Baptist Church. And Rev. Rick Warren, author of The Purpose Driven Life, preaches to 16,000 people a week at Saddleback Church in Lake Forest, California.

We are witnessing stockbrokers, corporate executives, elected officials and others transition from those jobs to the church, and bringing the skills that made them a success in the secular world to the church. In fact, if you visit many churches today, you'll find marketing and communications teams coming up with all sorts of interesting ways of reaching the unsaved and the unchurched.

> The growth of the church is clearly a result of the word of God speaking directly to the needs of today's people.

The growth of the church is clearly a result of the word of God speaking directly to the needs of today's people — average, ordinary but God-led people.

As I think about these awesome men and women of God, I just can't but help but think of Peter and John causing the powerful men of the Sanhedrin to scratch their heads, wondering how these two, non-descript individuals could be causing such a ruckus and winning so many souls.

Prior to accepting Jesus' call to follow him into ministry, Peter and John were fishermen. Frankly, none of the apostles held positions that were held in high esteem.

They were the polar opposite of the men of the Sanhedrin. Some biblical scholars considered them to be the supreme council among the Jews. Eugene Peterson's *The Message* Bible translation said they were *"the rulers, religious leaders, religion scholars…everybody who was anybody was there."*

These men were held in high regards, but Peter and John didn't care about their titles and positions in the community. *"Filled with the Holy Spirit"* (Acts

4:8), all they were concerned about was preaching the news of Jesus with courage, boldness and clarity.

What is important about this scripture is that God needs men and women of faith who are not concerned with how many degrees they have or who they know. God is in need of spiritual warriors who will witness and disciple, near and far.

In churches across the country, well-meaning people are being stifled from using their spiritual gifts because church leaders have not given them the authority to spread the word of God. One of the problems with the kingdom of God is that we seem to limit ourselves because of fleshly standards.

Look, God doesn't care if all you have is a high school diploma. The Lord isn't worried about you being able to rattle off the great philosophers of the world. What is of utmost of concern to God is whether you and I have made the effort to study our Bible and live a life for Jesus Christ.

I am confident that if Jesus can pluck 12 men out of obscurity and they could transform the world, then you can be used in a mighty way.

# What are you prepared to do?

*Text focus: 1 Kings: 18-21*
***

1 Kings 18:21; "Elijah went before the people and said, 'How long will you waver between two opinions? If the Lord is God, follow Him; but if Baal is God, follow him. But the people said nothing."

Anyone who knows me will tell you that I am an absolute movie buff. My house is littered with videos and DVDs of the films that have captured my fancy. I've watched these movies over and over, seemingly finding something new and interesting in each viewing. But the one flick that is one of my all-time favorites is *"The Untouchables."*

Made in 1987, *The Untouchables* stars Kevin Costner, Sean Connery and Robert DeNiro. Costner plays Elliott Ness, a U.S. Treasury agent who was assigned the task of bringing down mob boss, Al Capone (DeNiro). Connery plays a fictional, streetwise police officer, Jim Malone, who is one of the few on the force who isn't being bribed to turn the other cheek as Capone's henchman break the law by importing liquor during Prohibition.

Shortly after arriving in Chicago, things aren't going so swell for Ness (Costner). Capone is eluding him at every turn and the Chicago police are of no help. Frustrated, he meets with Malone (Connery) in a church to discuss the situation.

Malone doesn't mince any words.

"You said you wanted to know how to get Capone...do you really want to get him? You see what I'm saying? What are you prepared to do?"

"Everything within the law."

God is tired of us playing around. It's time to take a stand. It's time to make a decision.

"And then what are you prepared to do?"

It seems that the baby-faced Ness thought he was trying to mediate a dispute between tee times at the country club. He doesn't fully comprehend what it means to take down Capone, that's why Malone wants to see how far he is willing to go to win the war.

Putting this in a spiritual context, are you willing to win the spiritual war that you're presently in?

Evil lurks around every corner. Our children are being assaulted at every turn with images that are corrupting their minds. Pornography is reaching into the homes of men and women and tearing up marriages. Our single men and women are succumbing with temptation all around them, and not heeding the advice of Paul and living their life for God.

Are you in any one of these groups? If so, what are you prepared to do? That's essentially the question God is asking as we read this scripture.

Here is Elijah, the lone remaining Godly prophet in the land, standing on Mount Carmel to confront the prophets of Baal. He is providing them a final opportunity to turn away from sin and put their lives in the hands of the Lord.

How many times have you had to ask yourself this very same question? You know you were embarking on doing wrong, and God had given you the free will to make a decision, so you just say, "Hey, if I do wrong, God will forgive me anyhow."

Maybe some of you are holy rollers and think that this scripture doesn't speak to you. If so, let me put this another way to make it plain.

According to *The Quest Study Bible*, "Baal was the Canaanite fertility god believed to be responsible for germinating crops, increasing flocks and adding children to the community; best known of the Canaanite gods."

It's important to remember that during biblical days, Israel was largely an agricultural country and their survival was dependant on working the land. If there was a famine, crops were non-existent and starvation would rule the day. So when they were faced with problems in the land, they would turn away from God for help and pray to gods like Baal to cause it to run so their crops could grow and flocks could flourish, which in turn would help them eat, live and expand their families. In other words, they looked to Baal to provide them sustenance to keep living and breathing.

With this in mind, what is your Baal? What is it that you look to in place of God to ensure that you live a fruitful life?

Again, get off your high horse and be honest. How many times have you put aside your prayer life or chose to skip church or some other ministry function because you said your work was more important? As far as you were concerned, Bible study wasn't on the to-do-list because networking with potential clients would give you a better shot at landing that promotion.

Is money your Baal? Is tithing less important for you to buy the right house, car or taking the ultimate vacation?

For someone else, his or her Baal is sex. Despite what the scriptures says, they insist that going a day without sleeping with someone else is impossible. Nothing else is on their minds but hooking up with the next man or woman.

In essence, our Baal is that one thing that gives ultimate pleasure and adds fuel to our lives. Without it, we believe that we are nothing.

Elijah knew that was the understanding of the prophets of Baal. They didn't care one bit about God bringing the children of Israel out of Egypt. I'm sure they said. Baal will get us through the day (I'll bet a parent is shaking their head right now because their child has said that "momma or daddy, your God ain't my God").

This is the kind of thinking that often leads many astray. Instead of turning to God to be our provider and giver of all things, we choose to resort to the madness of the world and follow the game plan of Satan.

I can't tell you how many times I've talked to friends who thought the answer to their Godly marriage turning sour was running to the courthouse and getting a divorce. You may be celebrating being free of that man or woman, but you can bet Satan is also jumping up and down for getting between what God put asunder. Divorce, other than on biblical grounds, is turning to Baal and following Baal.

When we grow frustrated, angry or scared with the way our lives are going, we often turn away from God and seek to find solace in other sources.

That is surely a recipe of disaster.

The Lord is tired of Christians sitting on the fence, straddling the ways of the world and the spiritual realm.

God is tired of us playing around. It's time to take a stand. It's time to make a decision.

# Your trial is
# your testimony

Prior to giving a speech in Birmingham in 2002, the person who was going to introduce me asked if there was anything in my past that I didn't want people to know about. Without hesitation I replied, "No." He was baffled by my answer, so I explained to him why I felt that way. All too often, we like to keep silent about those negative, bad and demoralizing things that happen in our life. Divorce, domestic violence, abortion, adultery, abandonment, poverty and incest are some of the issues many people have had to endure as children or adults. The pain of those circumstances are so deep that many of us place them in a cave and roll a rock in front of it, always hoping they are never resurrected. And if we are in a situation where those topics are discussed, we either change the subject, get up from the table and leave, or sit in absolute silence, while tearing ourselves up on the inside.

Even some of the holiest of Christians do that. So many of us have prayed to God to redeem us, save us and deliver us from our predicament and restore that which was lost. Yet we want to keep our mouths silent when we have been delivered. Why? Didn't Jesus tell Legion (Mark 5:19) to go and tell his family what the Lord did for him? Legion could have chosen to not discuss the 2,000 demons that possessed him, but Jesus said to go forth and tell the good news of his deliverance.

What kind of Legion circumstance have you endured? And when you were extracted from your situation, did you go silent and not tell the people what God did for you?

By remaining silent you may be withholding vital information that will deliver someone from a bad situation.

There are countless individuals in the world who are going through difficult situations and they have no place to turn. They don't have a proper relationship with Christ and have no understanding of scripture, so telling them to read the Bible is meaningless.

You are required to inform them of your deliverance by telling them the good news of how the Lord blessed you, revived you and sanctified you. That requires you to tell your story — the whole story. That's right — the good, the bad and the ugly.

In Jeremiah 1, God tells the prophet, "*You must go to everyone I send you to and say whatever I command you. Do not be afraid of them, for I am with you and will rescue you.*"

Instead of being afraid of "them," so many of us are actually afraid of ourselves. Be honest. We think that our friends, church members and coworkers will look at us strangely if we talk openly and honestly about a marriage that went sour, or being addicted to drugs and alcohol. The wonderful facade that we have put up keeps others from knowing the real us.

Yet God knows us. He knows what we think, what we suffered and what got us through the turmoil.

If you are one of those individuals, understand that your trial is your testimony. By remaining silent you may be withholding vital information that will deliver someone from a bad situation.

As I told the gentleman in Birmingham, I'm not afraid to discuss those things that I used to do or the bad marriage I was in. My moments of anger must be discussed in the context of my focus on love and kindness. The doubts of my faith have been replaced with rock-bed faith. I refuse to be a prisoner to my past circumstances because I know that God delivered me healed me and made me whole, so therefore I owe it to myself to follow the Lord and speak a word of encouragement into someone else's life.

Make the effort to not just be a churchgoer, but to be a living witness and disciple on behalf of God. Remember, you story is one of power, purpose and possibilities. And it may be just the antidote to setting your friend or family member on the path to knowing and experiencing the fullness of God.

# Speaking the truth,
# no matter what

*Text focus: Jeremiah 1:7-8*

***

There is nothing like a bright light thrust upon our failings and weaknesses. Criticism in any form is something so many of us despise because those issues and sinful acts we are engaged in are being exposed for others to see.

Many of us would do anything not to be criticized for our weaknesses, especially if they are made public. It often feels like we are being attacked, which often forces us to go on the defensive.

For those who are married or were married, how vicious did you respond when your spouse pointed out, harped on or shined a light on your shortcomings? Even if that person was responding in anger to something you said, we cannot discount the truths they spoke.

We have the same reaction when our parents or siblings take us to task. I know some people who won't even speak to their family members because of this same issue.

Such criticism is not welcomed, even within a spiritual context. In many churches today, pastors are increasingly afraid to tackle tough topics for fear of alienating their flock. If someone gets mad, they may refuse to drop their money into the basket, or worse, leave the church. These concerns have only been magnified because churches have become such huge enterprises. Pastors and church leaders are about as sensitive to criticism from members as McDonald's is about customer service.

But it must be understood that the pastor, prophet or church elder isn't supposed to make nice all the time. Church is not designed to be a place where we go to hear stuff that we like to hear and not be challenged in our faith. Scripture is designed to help us, assist us and also hold us accountable for what are supposed to do.

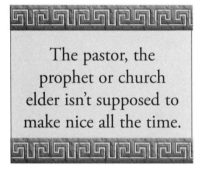

The pastor, the prophet or church elder isn't supposed to make nice all the time.

If Jesus is the head of the church, as so many of us say over and over, then we must use Him as an example when it comes to saying what needs to be said.

Jesus was unafraid to speak the truth when it needed to be spoken. The same can be said of Jeremiah. When God came to Jeremiah as a child, he instructed him to speak the truth, regardless of what others say and do. Can you imagine God entrusting you with this responsibility?

Jesus tells us in Matthew not to judge others. Yet we are also required to speak against sin when we confront it. In order to do so, that means we must work diligently in our spiritual lives to live as much of a sin-free life as we possibly can. It goes without saying that the man who is engaged in adultery doesn't have a moral leg to stand on when he calls out another friend. If he has repented, yes, but if he continues to sin, then he is simply being a hypocrite.

There are some right now who are saying, "I am never one to criticize because anybody can say bad things about me." That is true, but the question to ask yourself is this: "Would they be correct with their complaints?" It's easy to allege false statements against someone, but can they be proven to be correct? If not, then we can chalk that up to simple jealousy.

It is so much easier for us to continue doing what we've been doing, wallowing in our own little world and not being bothered by those around us who are engaged in sinful behavior. But we owe it to ourselves, and those who we love, to speak out against what we know is wrong. If a man is verbally abusing his wife, we should not sit idly by and say, "That's their business and not mine." By putting on the armor of God, we are able to minister to that man, show him with scripture why his behavior is wrong and properly show him how to handle his anger.

If your sister in Christ is constantly abusing the finances of her household, you should go to her and explain what stewardship is and how we are supposed to take care of what God has blessed us with. This might require you to get your house in order. Good! There's no sense in the two of you being out of order!

Remember, all criticism is not bad. When done with love, care and respect (read Psalms 19:14), we may just be helping someone to get back on the right path and live a more spiritually balanced life.

# Shake it up

*Text focus: Text focus: Matthew 21:12-13;*
*Mark 11:15-17; Luke 19:45-46*
***

Jesus has often been portrayed as a meek and docile figure that never got upset or angry at the circumstances around him. But the reality is that Jesus was God in the flesh, and as such, got sick and tired of the mess he had to deal with.

We see the evidence of this in our text. When returning to the temple in Jerusalem, Jesus had reached his breaking point with the individuals who were treating the house of prayer as a spiritual Wal-Mart; selling anything and everything without regard to the true purpose of the temple. That's when Jesus reached his breaking point and started flipping tables and benches, and kicking out the folks who were buying and selling their goods. "My house will be called a house of prayer but you are making it a 'den of robbers,'" he said.

I'm sure everyone, including his followers, was shocked to see Jesus behave in such a manner. I can imagine Peter saying, "Uh, oh! The Lord has lost his mind!" Jesus recognized that as long as the temple was corrupted, the people would continue to be deprived of what God wanted them to know and understand.

Many of us should take a cue from Jesus and begin to turn over the table and benches of individuals who are robbing us of our joy and happiness.

These folks — friends, family, co-workers and church folk — are "spiritual robbers" who are only concerned about taking from us instead of investing in us. They are destroying our temples — the body — by their negative influences.

> Take a cue from Jesus and begin to turn over the table and benches of individuals who are robbing us of our joy and happiness.

Take a moment and read 1 Corinthians 3:16: *"Don't you know that you yourselves are God's temple and that God's Spirit lives in you?"*

We must be honest with ourselves and begin to think of the people who are having a negative influence on our lives. It might be a boss or a job that is weighing you down, and constantly keeping you depressed or angry. You might be in a church where the theology being preached doesn't fully conform to God's word, and where the members are more interested in deifying the pastor as opposed to living God's word. As a result, you are being robbed of the spiritual food you need to survive in this chaotic world.

Maybe you are stuck in a relationship that batters you mentally, physically and spiritually. I know several folks, men and women, who are consumed with having a warm body to lay next to, as opposed to being with someone who is willing to love them according to God's will. This is not the way anyone should live! First Corinthians 6:19 says, *"Do you not know that your body is a temple of the Holy Spirit, who is in you, whom you have received from God? You are not your own; you were bought at a price. Therefore honor God with your body."*

If this is you, then follow the lead of Jesus and begin to shake some things up in your life. Turn over the tables of the robbers around you and begin to follow a path where Jesus' teaching is first and foremost. As long as you are stuck in a situation where your spirit is being deprived of what is rightfully yours, you will continue to walk around in a state of despair.

But read the text again. The onus isn't just on turning over the tables of the robbers. You must also stop going to the table of the robbers. That's right. There is a responsibility you must assume in not destroying your temple through your bad decisions. If you know that the man or woman in your life is taking rather than giving, stop calling them at 1 a.m. when you are feeling lonely. If you know in your spirit that you aren't being fed at that church, find a new home.

Don't continue to give them your tithes, your energy and your talents, and then get upset with the lack of spiritual direction in your life. If that job of yours is driving you up the wall, devise an exit strategy that allows you to find a more fulfilling job. There is a dual responsibility, we must be willing to shake up and throw out the robbers in our lives, and we must also not stop at their tables if we see them again.

We can pray all day for God to improve our situation. And I am confident that the Lord will do His part and answer our prayers according to His will. But we also must do our part and take proactive measures to change a bad situation. Jesus did it, and through the strength he exhibited, you can too.

# Learn to just be

*Text focus: Psalm 4:4*

\*\*\*

In an age of Palm pilots, two-way pagers, cell phones, e-mail, faxes and constant communication devices, the freedom that they purport to offer us tend to shrink our world and bring about tremendous stress and strain.

No longer do we put work away at night or the weekend. Monday through Friday has now turned into Monday through Sunday. Vacations are pushed aside for the "power weekends" or quickie getaways.

I can't sit here and be hypocritical; I've succumbed to all that the world's "conveniences" have to offer. In 2001 or 2002, I felt like I was on the treadmill of life and there was no stop or pause button. As editor of BlackAmericaWeb.com and news editor of *Savoy* Magazine, I was working on countless stories, doing interviews, taking photos and filing them. Then I took the audio from the interviews and filed stories for the American Urban Radio Networks. Sandwiched between all of that was a book I was working on trying to finish (*Speak Brother: A Black Man's View of America*), responding to the countless e-mails I get every day from readers and co-workers, then trying to deal with the other businesses I'm involved in.

My wife had to deal with the same, she was constantly going back and forth to Houston to work with a day spa we were helping to open, and flying across the country preaching and teaching at various conferences and retreats. We probably saw one another five days for the entire month of February!

Just when I felt like the world was closing in around me, I had to come to the conclusion to put the brakes on.

When we are so busy with life's demands sometimes that's hard for us to do. We act as if we don't have time for the things that matter because we must get that project done now, and move on to the next thing, because that deadline is looming. Yet all that does is cause our life to speed up and get faster and faster and faster. And by doing so, we are putting our health at risk, our relationships with wives, husbands and kids on the line, and of course, our relationship with God.

Yes, even God gets put on the backburner. Don't be so holy and think that He doesn't. You may go to church on Sunday and possibly Wednesday night Bible study, but those important times when you need to sit still and be with God are even greater than going through the motions of church. We often wait until we are through with all the things in our day before we give God His time. And then we are so tired we head off to bed, knowing full well we are wrong for neglecting our spiritual life.

Like in so many areas of life, we must take our cue from Jesus when it comes to sitting down and just dwelling within the spirit of the Lord. How many times throughout Scripture have we taken note of Jesus getting away from the people, and even his disciples, to go and commune with God? Jesus knew and understood that in his humanly form he did not have the power and strength to deal with the constant teaching and preaching that he was required to do.

Even Jesus would sit down and just "be." There would be nothing for him to do, no place for him to go, no person for him to counsel. He would just sit down and dwell in the presence of God in order to gain the wisdom and knowledge he needed to deal with the forces in life.

You may be saying, "Man, you're nuts! I've got these kids, a job where my boss is acting crazy, a husband or wife that is getting on my last nerves, a sick brother or sister and the pressures of bills, bills, bills. I can't handle it!" And I understand that, but you must slow down and realize that the pressure will affect every part of you, including your sanity. Internalizing all of that nonsense can also affect your health. Stress often causes other maladies to harm our body.

I love the fact that Jesus would just get away. Today, there are lots of commercials that pump up flying away from the weekend and leaving your cares at home. But all that does is increase your credit card debt and leave you in more trouble. If you can do it, great. But for those who can't, make the effort to create a quiet time or even a silent weekend. Unplug all of the televisions in the house, don't answer or use the phone, and focus on getting inside of yourself. I know you may really want to grab that e-mail or pick up the newspaper, but don't. Discipline yourself to follow the strict standard you have set. If it's a silent weekend, make an effort not to talk. It will be hard to do so, but again, you are shutting yourself from the world and getting inside of yourself to learn more about you and to move into a closer relationship with God.

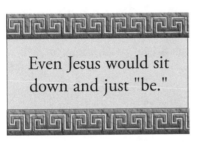

Even Jesus would sit down and just "be."

When Jesus would go away to meditate, I don't believe he was in a state of prayer the entire time (Matthew 8:1; Matthew 14:13; Matthew 14:23). I'm sure he may have been walking around or sitting down and just looking, breathing and thinking. It's amazing how much we can learn when our minds aren't occupied with artificial noise and we concentrate on ourselves. How refreshing is it to take a walk along the beach or simply down the street, looking at the sun, clouds, grass and other elements of nature. I recall a year or so ago running out of gas and having to flag some folks down. It was cold and windy, but at the moment I should have begun to fret, I looked across an open field and saw this beautiful image of the grass swaying back and forth as the light of the moon reflected on it. Mind you, I was worried about getting some gas, but all I could do was stop in my tracks and see the beauty of God at what I thought was an inopportune time. But I guess the Lord wanted me to recognize his majesty in my time of peril. (Now that's a word for someone whose situation is far direr, but it can release you from your situation!)

Practice the art of release. Walking around with pent up frustrations is hard. You feel lethargic, it drags you down, and let's be honest, you aren't the greatest person to be around when that happens! You must learn to just let some stuff go. There are many issues that are way beyond your control. No matter what you think, you will get through it.

Finally, learn to cast them upon the Lord.

There have been countless times when my mind was put to rest, and my body at ease, when I called out to the Lord and asked him to deal with my situation. That allowed me to free myself from the pain and agony and "just be."

The art of just "being" is that of allowing the madness around you to continue while you keep your head all about you. It may mean driving down the road with no music playing, and the cell phone not attached to your ear.

It could also be achieved by sitting in your living room as you watch your kids play in the background, with their enthusiasm for life exuding all throughout the house. It may mean resting your head on your spouse's chest on the couch or in the bed, thinking and smiling about the person who loves you so much.

It may even be as simple of sitting in your living room, prayer room or bathroom, relaxing and breathing as you take in each blessing the Lord has provided for you.

If your life is moving out of control and you are trying to play catch-up, simply stop, pause, reflect and make the effort to "just be" and to live in the moment. It may cause you to appreciate all that you have just a little bit more.

# In due time

*Text focus: John 2*

\*\*\*

Many of you have written e-mails over the last few weeks, thanking me for one of my columns that have blessed you in some form or fashion. But a familiar refrain in a lot of them has to do with you praying and praying and praying, and not receiving an answer to those prayers.

So many of you have said that you have become frustrated and sometimes despondent over your situation not changing. On one hand you were thanking and blessing God, but on the other you were somewhat questioning Him because of a lack of closure to your dilemma.

As I was getting ready for my nightly dose of reading three chapters of the Bible, God told me to skip what I had planned on reading and go on to John 2. That is where Jesus performs his first miracle, including turning water into wine.

His mother, who informed him that the wine at the wedding has run out, approached Jesus.

*"Dear woman, why do you involve me?"* Jesus replied. *"My time has not yet come."*

According to *The Quest* Study Bible, Jesus' statement of his time not yet coming refers to his coming death. It says: "Jesus clearly states that his time to be revealed as the Messiah and crucified as the sacrificial Lamb has not yet arrived. Completely in tune with the will of God, Jesus was waiting for the right moment to fulfill the purpose for which God had sent him into the world."

Yet as I read, my spirit began to cry out that his statement can also be applied to your particular situation. You are facing something that is so critical and tough that you just want God to remove the yoke from around your neck and allow you to be pain-free. The problem may have to do with a divorce, child custody battle, finances, and dissension in the workplace, jealously at church or any number of problems. You been praying, fasting, tithing, reading your daily Word and doing all you can to leave it at the altar, but it continues to weigh you down. There are some days you just don't feel like fighting anymore.

But even in the midst of your pain, as the Kurt Carr Singers say, "Jesus kept me." My spirit also said that although you have been a faithful servant, the time has not come for Him to intervene on your behalf. There are some lessons that still must come out of your walk through the valley. He will respond, but in due time.

All too often we revel in the blessing without realizing that the true blessing was the journey. Isn't our testimony so much sweeter when we talk about all that we went through to overcome? We don't focus on how great it all is today. We cherish telling others how we survived when it felt like we were in that lion's den with Daniel. The blessing is great, but our story is so much more awesome when we share with others the pain of the journey and how we came through the experience!

The Holy Spirit simply wants me to let you know that it isn't time for Jesus to show up and show out. Yes, He can do it at anytime He chooses, but God needs for some of you to continue in your present posture and maintain your faith and your obedience. Your faith is being tested. Your love for Him is being tested. Your ability to trust Him is being tested. You are being made tougher by your circumstances. Even as you continue to praise Him and call on Him, He sees your love for Him because you do it in the midst of pain.

I can recall a situation in 1999 that almost brought me to my knees with doubt, anger, despair and lack of willpower. My marriage had ended, my job was completely unsatisfactory and I was feeling alone and hurt. For two consecutive weeks the Lord woke me up between 5 a.m. and 5:30 a.m. and said, "Patience."

> We revel in the blessing without realizing that the true blessing was the journey.

That's right. Each day I would hear the same voice. It was like clockwork that this was happening. Anyone who knows me knows that I'm not the most patient person in the world. But he would say, "Patience. Now go back to sleep." I wanted to tell God to holla at me around 9 a.m., but I guess he wanted me to get the point!

I didn't know what the issues were. I had no idea what was in my path, but clearly he wanted me to have patience for whatever was coming.

The next two years were painful as all get out. I left my job, had a new house (used all of my savings, but again, he instructed me to do so and I was obedient), the bills were stacking up and he kept saying, "I will supply all your needs."

As I continued on this journey God kept instructing me to read the Word, study the Word and focus on Him. I was in the middle of a battle, yet God was telling me to sit on the sideline and let Him be God. I was praying for a job to replace the lost income. I was dipping in blessed oil everyday, anointing my head, hands and eyes and doing everything I could to get out of the situation. You name it, I tried it. Yet none of it worked. That's because Roland was trying to operate on a level that was not my area to focus on.

I applied for job after job that, if I removed 90 percent of my resume, I should have still gotten without any problem. But the Lord said, "That's not for you. Wait on me and I've got you." I had to learn that my schedule mattered nothing to God. My life's goals and ambitions were not necessarily His life's goals and ambitions for me. I had to surrender myself, lay it all on the altar and say, "Lord, do with me as you wish." The moment I professed those words my life began to change. I began to see things in a whole different dimension. I would read Scripture and other things would be revealed. I began to accept my spiritual gifts of discernment and the prophetic. In other words, I allowed myself to be used as God's vessel.

Let me encourage you: Your situation is the hardest thing you've ever had to face. It has brought you tears and left you feeling empty, emotionless, and downright angry. But, as Dr. Ron Elmore says, you are in the waiting room of life. God needs you to wait just a little bit in order for Him to make the necessary arrangements for your blessing. Yes, God can snap his fingers and make things happen, just like Jesus could have stood up and turned the water into wine. But He had to do it quietly because it wasn't his time to reveal himself yet.

Now is not the time for you to be removed from your situation. Now is not the time for Jesus to reveal himself. What you are learning in your trial of life will one day be your testimony. Take the time to learn the lesson, ask God to reveal what you need to be learning in your present predicament and allow God to move on your behalf in His due time.

# Pledge ruling doesn't remove God from America

So a federal panel in California has ruled that the Pledge of Allegiance is unconstitutional because God is mentioned. Good, maybe we can now focus on the Word of God rather than the word in a pledge that has no sustaining value to an individual's life.

Christian conservatives are up in arms, but they didn't mind President George W. Bush allowing them to scoop out of the government trough with his faith-based initiatives. Liberals are hailing the decision because of the separation of church and state, but when they were scared out of their wits after September 11, they were in churches and on their knees, praying for God to keep them safe.

When the ruling was first made in June, a collective gasp could be heard around the country. Both political parties sprang into action condemning the decision by the 9th U.S. Circuit Court of Appeals, one of the most liberal in the country. Republicans and Democrats stood side by side to express shock at the decision. The U.S. Senate broke from their regular business to pass a resolution 99-0 condemning the ruling. Even Fox News Channel threw out any pretense of balance and fairness by posting the photo of the lead judge, as well as his office phone number, on the screen all day. I guess the "we report, you decide" moniker they use also got thrown out the window.

Ministers, politicians and regular day folk have continuously lamented that this nation is going down the drain because of its moral decay and failure to follow God's commands. But why do followers of God sit silently by at the injustices of life? The Catholic Church turns the other way when boys are molested, Sunday at 10 a.m. is the most segregated hour of the week, Southern Baptists want women to stay in their place by not being pastors and many of us have accepted a "do-whatever-you-like" mentality at any time.

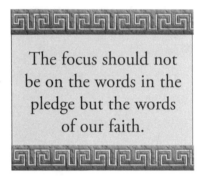

The focus should not be on the words in the pledge but the words of our faith.

We are a country that was founded on the love of God, yet we were also founded on religious freedom and the ability to choose to partake in it or not. America wasn't supposed to be a place of religious persecution; we are just as entitled to praise or ignore God. But let this be clear: there is not a law in the land or a big enough paycheck that would prevent me from saying a prayer any time I want to. If I choose to commune with God, I would do it right then and there, regardless of what someone else says.

We don't need a Pledge of Allegiance to show that we are a God-fearing nation, and I don't have to throw someone in jail for burning a flag. My love for America will burn brighter than any flame that sprouts up from a burning piece of cloth.

The focus should not be on the words in the pledge but the words of our faith. I am married to a pastor, and I bow down to one being, and that is Jesus Christ. My eyes are on Him; not some dudes wearing black robes in San Francisco or even the President of the United States. If you want to take the pledge away, go right ahead. But the day you want to prevent me from praying to my God, then we're going to have some issues.

What so many of us have gotten confused about is that we are caught in the trap of words rather than the Holy Spirit. That's right: spirit. The spirit of

God should be on us, in us and work around us. But no, we would much prefer to spend time and energy crying over the pledge being declared unconstitutional.

Parents, don't let the pledge be the only time your child says God. Sit, study and pray with your son and daughter. Faith in God — and not the Pledge of Allegiance — will get them through terror warnings, natural disasters and the ordinary troubles in this journey called life.

# Marriage: A gift from God

Second only to the birth of a child, marriage could very well be the most precious gift from God.

When you think of what it means to join in covenant with a man or woman under the direction and authority of the Holy Spirit it is absolutely awesome. Scripture speaks of the issue of oneness when a man and woman unite in holy matrimony, and it's imperative that we uphold and speak positively about this institution.

With so many people divorcing for a number of reasons, you may ask: "Why in the world would he want to sit here and write a series of essays on marriage?"

The answer is simple: because the Holy Spirit said so. And I don't operate under the authority of man but am obedient to where God is leading me.

It must be understood that the series on marriage is not meant to be "this-is-my-way-and-the-heck-with-you." The aim is to speak to many of the issues in marriage — communication, intimacy, love, honor, respect — and that thorny topic we hate to discuss, submission.

As a child of God and a believer in Jesus Christ, I can only use scripture as the foundation for discussing marriage because marriage is a blessing from God.

Therefore, the principles and issues discussed will all be biblically based.

Now, it makes no sense to have a discussion about marriage and not offer much needed resources to help you through your situation.

When I was divorced in 1999, the Lord placed on my heart a number of books that He wanted me to read. The last thing I wanted to be doing was read those books, but as He told me, "I am going to be sending people to you who are experiencing marriage difficulties, and I want you to be prepared." But I acted like Moses and said, "Not me!" Then I was simply told that even when Moses didn't want to submit to God's orders, he was delicately told he had no choice.

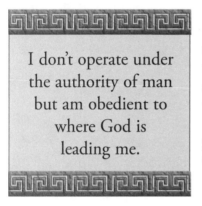

I don't operate under the authority of man but am obedient to where God is leading me.

What many of these books did was provide different perspectives that were timely and necessary. Not only was I coming out of a divorce, but I was also about to go back into the world of "being on the market" and I needed to get the understanding of how to date as a Christian and deal with all the temptations that I would be facing.

**Suggested reading:**

*I Dont Want Delilah, I Need You!: What a Woman Needs to Know and What a Man Needs to Understand* by Bishop Eddie L. Long

*The Five Love Languages: How to Express Heartfelt Commitment to Your Mate* by Gary Chapman

*Liberated Through Submission: God's Design for Freedom in All Relationships!* by P.B. Wilson

*Point Man: How a Man Can Lead His Family* by Steve Farrar

*Standing Tall: How a Man Can Protect His Family* by Steve Farrar

# Marriage: Divorce
# is not an option

*Text focus: Ephesians 6*
***

U sing divorce as the starting point for a series on marriage may strike some as a bit odd, but it actually makes sense considering the trials and tribulations one may face in marriage often leads one or both parties to call it quits.

We live in a society that has taken the view that marriage is just about the same as buying a car: if we don't like the color, how it drives or want an upgrade, we'll just roll back to the dealership and get a new model.

Recent statistics show that nearly half of all marriages in the United States end in divorce, and Christians are not exempt from that. Divorce is running rampant through churches, from the pulpit to the pew. A few years ago it got so out of hand in several counties in Oklahoma — the divorce rate among Christians had soared to 65 percent — that a number of pastors launched an all-out assault against divorce. Many of the initiatives included preaching on the issue of marriage, the covenant, commitment and forgiveness, as well as requiring all prospective brides and grooms to go through six months of counseling prior to taking the walk down the aisle.

# Listening to the Spirit Within

All too often when couples get married, they stand at the altar to recite vows and pledge to love one another unconditionally before friends, family, their pastor and of course, God. The vows include to love one another for richer and for poorer, in sickness and in health, and for better or for worse.

Yet for many it's more like for better and for better. When the first sign of trouble begins, too many of us quickly run because we don't want to go through the hard work that is necessary to make our marriages better. It's so much easier to quit than it is to persevere through the difficult days.

A few years ago a woman once told me, "If I have to work that hard for a marriage, I don't want it." That woman was my first wife, and that marriage dissolved in June 1999 after six years. I refused to even participate in the divorce filing because I didn't believe in it. The issues she raised as reasons for the divorce were so small that they could have easily been resolved. Sitting before my pastor, I said that I was willing to do anything and everything to save the marriage. But when you have selfish motives and live a life where "I-my" rules your thought process instead of "we-us-our," then divorce will be the end result. I even refused to sign the divorce papers unless her attorney added a statement that said I did not believe the reasons cited were worthy of a divorce. Why? Because until the end of time that divorce decree will exist. And if the children of my yet-to-be-conceived children ever did some research on me and came across the document, I want them to know that I wasn't down with the cause.

A little more than 15 months later I remarried, and when I stood at that aisle with my bride, the thought of divorce never entered into my mind. For me, it was, has and never will be an option. I refuse to speak it, think about it or even joke about the subject. There is no doubt that once you call something forth and speak it, evil forces then know what is in your mind and heart, and will seek to place temptations to make divorce a reality.

Lest any of us continue to live in marriages according to the world, scripture tells us that God hates divorce. Read that again: God HATES divorce. God doesn't justify it, explain it or even excuse it. Malachi 2:16 (NIV) says: "*Has not the Lord made them one? In flesh and spirit they are his. And why one? Because he was seeking Godly offspring. So guard yourself in your spirit, and do not break faith with the wife of your youth. 'I hate divorce,' says the Lord God of Israel."*

Skip on over to Matthew 19 where Jesus was asked specifically about divorce. What did he say? *"Moses permitted you to divorce your wives because your hearts were hard. But it was not this way from the beginning. I tell you that anyone who divorces his wife, except for marital unfaithfulness, and marries another woman commits adultery...Not everyone can accept this word, but only those to whom it has been given. For some are eunuchs because they were born that way, others were made that way by men and others have renounced marriage because of the kingdom of heaven. The one who can accept this should accept it."*

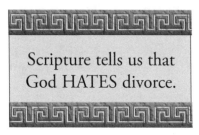

Scripture tells us that God HATES divorce.

## Hands off

"But what about domestic violence?" That was one of the questions bandied about on an online discussion I participated in in 2000. I chose not to participate because I was so swamped with work, but I then made the mistake of asking God the question. What did he do? Answer my question.

I said, "God, what about domestic violence? If adultery is the only reason, what about a woman who is being severely beaten by her husband? Is she supposed to stay in that kind of relationship?" Shortly after asking the question, He answered by asking me to turn to several scriptures. Keep in mind, I grew up Catholic and had no clue when it comes to the Bible — it's just not taught. So when the scriptures began to come to me, I knew it was all Him and not me.

God had me read Matthew and what Jesus said about divorce. Then I was told to turn to Ephesians 5:28 which says, *"In this same way, husbands ought to love their wives as their own bodies."* God then spoke to me and said that no man would knowingly abuse himself, and if so, he should not lay hands on a woman. Beating a woman is not Godly. You don't beat what you love. The Lord then had me to turn Jeremiah, where the issue of adultery was a large part of the book.

In Jeremiah 3:7, the Lord spoke the following to the prophet Jeremiah: *"I thought that after she had done all this she would return to me but she did not, and her unfaithful sister Judah saw it. I gave faithless Israel her certificate of divorce and sent her away because of all her adulteries. Yet I saw that her unfaithful sister Judah had no fear; she also went out and committed adultery.*

*Because Israel's immorality mattered so little to her, she defiled the land and committed adultery with stone and wood."*

I sat there dumbfounded. "Okay, Lord, what in the world does all of this mean?"

"You have it all confused Roland," the Lord said. "You and other humans have limited my Word to think that adultery only means to be unfaithful by having sex outside of the marriage." Even dictionary.com defines adultery as "voluntary sexual intercourse between a married person and a partner other than the lawful spouse."

But the Lord said, "No, adultery means to be unfaithful to the covenant that has been established between one another. When the children of Israel were unfaithful by turning their backs on me, they were committing adultery against me. As married Christians, you have chosen to commit adultery by not following the principles and guidelines that I laid down as it relates to marriage. By breaking those principles, you have committed adultery against the covenant. For every man who beats his wife, he is breaking the covenant established in Ephesians 5 and his wife has a right to divorce him accordingly."

I sat at my desk in amazement at what I heard. But instead of sitting back, I could only ask more questions. "But God, if that is the case, that means folks can run to the courts and file for divorce because we often break so many of the marriage principles beyond sex with an unlawful partner. There is anger, resentment, and not being good financial stewards, among other things. If what you are telling me is the case, then what in the heck does this mean for marriage?"

God then said, "You still don't get it. When the children of Israel committed adultery against me, my anger was strong. But I forgave the children over and over for their misdeeds. I only turned my back on them when their adultery grew so rampant that they had to be taught a lesson. But instead of being so quick to file divorce, what you should do is practice love and forgiveness. If I could forgive my children from turning away from me and worshipping other gods, then you and others can forgive your wives and husbands."

Talk about a blessing! I would suggest that in the case of domestic violence and other anger management issues, the wife should leave the home and impress upon her husband to get the proper counseling for his anger. No woman should stand before any man who chooses to be violent with her. But that wife, as well as those around her, should continually work to intercede and pray on behalf of the husband. The men of God in the church should not turn a blind eye, even if he is the deacon, head of the men's ministry or even the pastor himself. They should use their influence to speak to the man and work with him through his issues.

Likewise, women who verbally abuse their God-fearing spouses should also recognize the wrongs they commit. There are a number of well-meaning men who are constantly rundown by their wives. Many of these brothers operate quietly, yet are torn up on the inside as their self-esteem is attacked. Ladies read James 3, which speaks to the taming of the tongue. Your words should be used to uplift a man, not uproot him.

What we have to understand is that there are many people who have evil spirits that reside in them that they refuse to acknowledge. We must recognize that Satan doesn't want to see a single marriage work because that only gives God the glory. I am convinced that a strong family builds a strong church; a strong church builds a strong community; a strong community builds a strong city; a strong city builds a strong state; a strong state builds a strong nation; and a strong nation builds a strong world. We must access and accept the power of prayer by leaning on not our own understanding but in the power of the Holy Spirit. Then our marriages can be revived.

I have personally witnessed individuals who didn't tolerate domestic violence, but they also didn't run from the marriage. They believed that the man they were married to was set aside by God, and they earnestly prayed for a spirit of peace to overtake that man and truly make him an Ephesians man.

**Don't run from the problem**

There are many of you who don't have the problem of domestic violence, but the issues between you and your spouse are so difficult that you just want to throw you hands up and quit.

Don't.

Bishop Eddie L. Long, in his powerful book, *I Don't Want Delilah! I Need You*, told the story of his dad being an alcoholic. He said his mother wasn't aware of his drinking problem before they got married and was shocked to discover it. Her husband wasn't going to church and leading his family from a spiritual perspective. But she never badgered him, ridiculed him or left him.

What did she do? She prayed for him.

Long says every Sunday she would get the kids ready for church and "minister" to her husband. She didn't use her mouth to run down her husband, instead, she allowed her spirit to shine through and let God use her as the vessel to reach her husband. She chose to follow the ways described in 1 Peter 3: "Wives, in the same way be submissive to your husbands so that, if any of them do not believe the word, they may be won over without words by the behavior of their wives, when they see the purity and reverence of your lives." Mrs. Long chose to be a holy woman, allowing her "inner self, the unfading beauty of a gentle and quiet spirit" to determine how she dealt with her husband.

After several years of not going to church, Long wrote that his dad woke up one day, got dressed, grabbed his mother's hand and said, "Let's go to church." That day the preacher brought an uncompromising Word. Long's dad was convinced and he gave his life to Christ. His dad went on to found a number of other churches, and in the words of Bishop Long, had his mother not been a praying wife and a faithful wife, Long's daddy could not have accepted the Lord and later have done the Lord's work by touching thousands.

He also said a decision by Long's mother to leave could have prevented a small boy named Eddie to grow up and lead a 26,000-member congregation called New Birth Missionary Baptist Church near Atlanta.

Long's mother did try to leave once. She packed her bags and was headed out the door. But Long said he cried out to his mother and told her that if she left he would surely die. She heard the cry of her child, unpacked her bags and chose to fight for her marriage.

We cannot fall down and simply give up. If we do, so many of us don't know how many blessings we will leave behind.

## Light at the end of the tunnel

A story in *USA Today* reveals that divorce, despite what so many may say, doesn't necessarily make us happy.

The study, done by the prestigious University of Chicago, was commissioned by the Institute for American Values, a think-tank on the family. What it concluded was stunning:

• Of the 5,232 married adults studied, 645 were unhappy. Of that number, 167 of the unhappy were divorce within five years and 478 stayed married.

• The couples that stayed married said their marriages got stronger because they chose to work through their adversity instead of quitting.

• Staying married didn't trap unhappy spouses in violent relationships.

• The short-term problems of money, children and others issues subsided over time. The unhappy partners recognized their true feelings and changed their life for the betterment of the marriage.

What was startling is that many didn't turn to counselors. They often relied on their faith and personal views of marriage to work through their issues. (Many of the men didn't want to seek help because they didn't like spending money to have someone help solve their problems. We'll deal with that subject down the road).

Despite all of this, there will be many people who refuse to fight for their marriage and turn to divorce. Yes, my first wife wanted the divorce over my objections. I wasn't happy about it, but you can't force someone to stay married. It was a rough time for me personally, but I can say that in my time of difficulty I turned my life over to God and allowed Him to lead and guide me. There were many days I cried and was in pain, but the Lord stood by me and walked me through the process. God directed me to several resources that helped me through the difficulties.

And after going through all of that, God led me to a beautiful woman who is now my wife, the Rev. Jacquie Hood Martin.

Some of you may have remarried or are still looking for that Godly mate. Others may think, "It turned out good for him so why not me?" I'll simply say this: If you believe that the man or woman sitting next to you is the mate God truly led you to, then you should trust God. But remember: both people must work to save the marriage. Don't cave in and run from the problems. Commit yourself to building your relationship with Him and ask Him to show you what areas in your marriage can be improved. Practice forgiveness. Ask yourself some honest questions about what is making you unhappy and why the marriage is not fruitful. You may be scared to hear the answer, but sleeping in the same home as if you had a roommate is not marriage. You must step up to the plate and say, "Enough is enough!"

Remember to love your spouse unconditionally. If he or she is hostile to praying, fine. You pray. Do it day and night. And don't just pray for the marriage. Pray that God will touch, anoint and speak to your mate in a powerful way for the goodness of the relationship. Pray for a change in you so that a spirit of holiness can lead and guide you and not a spirit of vindictiveness.

We cannot and should not accept even one divorce. If Jesus can toss out the 2,000 demons in Legion, then surely he can remove the evil spirits that have invaded your circle of one. It all begins with you deciding to make the effort to get on the path of change.

Begin today to lean on Him, trust Him and not give in to the temptation. Remember, your marriage trial today can easily be a marriage testimony tomorrow.

# Marriage:
# The Covenant

There is no contract a lawyer could draw up that is more binding than God's covenant with his people. It is something that has lasting implications, is taken as serious as it is given, and is a direct blessing that comes from God.

Take the time and peruse through the Bible and see how often God makes a covenant with his people. In Genesis 9 he establishes a covenant with Noah, calling it an *"everlasting covenant."* Six chapters later a covenant is established between God and Abram (later changed to Abraham), saying he will be the father of many nations. The covenant was reiterated with Isaac and Jacob. God reminded Moses in Exodus 19 that he would remember His covenant if his commands were followed (another covenant was made in Exodus 34 with Moses).

Yet the covenant isn't solely between God and his people. Even biblical figures, following the lead of God, established covenants between one another. Jacob agrees to a covenant with Laban in Genesis 31:44 that will *"serve as a witness between us."* Jonathan, the son of Saul, made two covenants with David so that he would take care of Jonathan's family when the son of Jesse ascended to the throne as king.

And of course, the blood of Jesus was the ultimate covenant established between God and his wayward children.

In all, there are 287 references to the word covenant in the Bible (NIV). And one of the very first covenants established was that between man and woman. According to scripture, God pulled Eve out of Adam because He determined that man should not be alone. And He then so ordered in verse 24 that *"for this reason a man will leave his father and mother and be united to his wife, and they will become one flesh."* It is in this passage that oneness, the bedrock principle of the marriage covenant, was developed.

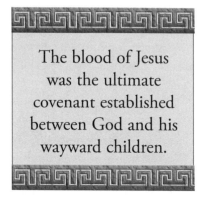

The blood of Jesus was the ultimate covenant established between God and his wayward children.

God clearly intended for man and woman to be in matrimony, but eventually because of man's sin, some chose not to follow the commands. That's why when Jesus spoke of marriage in Matthew 19, he alluded to some being made to marry while others have been given a spirit of singleness.

The importance of understanding covenant is critical because it is a personal testimony between one person and another that is not meant to be broken. Again, we are to take the covenant even more seriously than a contract for a job, car or anything else. God commanded his children to obey his covenant with all their heart or face his wrath. That wrath was necessary because we often take such covenants or "promises" with a not-so-serious attitude. That often leads us to have a blasé attitude about such matters. But God wants us to understand that His covenant is so powerful that he was willing to give us all that our hearts desire, IF we followed His commandments and obey His covenant. We are not to dismiss it casually. Yet we do the same thing the children of Israel did. Oh, they loved it when He made the covenant and led them out of Israel, yet they quickly got comfortable and forgot who led them out! And the same thing happens today. We promise God that we will do something — in other words we enter into a covenant with God — but when we are far removed from our pain, it's business as usual. If we blow off the covenant off with God, why should He uphold his end?

In Christian marriage, we stand before the altar and proclaim before friends and family that we will enter a covenant with our husband or wife to be with them until death do us part. God's intention is not for us to get divorced. We are to be with that person forever because we are entering into a lifelong covenant with them. God's covenant with Israel lasted 1,000 generations and beyond, so why do we call it quits after a couple of years? The covenant was supposed to be forever; I guess forever now has time limits at the first sign of trouble.

The covenant does not begin when we sign our name on the marriage certificate. It actually starts when we begin to speak covenant-affirming words. In Deuteronomy 29, God confirmed the covenant *"with an oath."* Folks, the words we recite are not merely words that we are speaking. It's not happy talk or chit-chat. They are serious words that we are to abide by.

The vows vary. Some people choose to write their own while others rely on scripture, such as 1 Corinthians 13. Remember, there is no set marriage vow. The key is that you do exactly as you say you will, according to what God has set down for marriage.

**Don't break your word**

As we know from reading scripture, Israel went back on the covenant God established with them time and time again. Unfortunately, there is reward when the covenant is followed and punishment when a covenant is forgotten.

We'll begin with the punishment.

In Deuteronomy 4 God warns Israel about their possible punishment for disobedience: *"But if you will not listen to me and carry out all these commands, and if you reject my decrees and abhor my laws and fail to carry out all my commands and so violate my covenant, then I will do this to you: I will bring upon you sudden terror, wasting diseases and fever that will destroy your sight and drain away your life. You will plant seed in vain, because your enemies will eat it."*

I don't know about you but that is a rough thing one must go through if we disobey the covenant. Now let's break it down as to how it applies to marriage.

"*I will bring sudden terror.*" How does it feel when your husband or wife broke the marriage covenant? Did you feel as if you marriage was under attack and all would end? Being beaten by their husband or wife, both physically and mentally, has terrorized some. Others have been killed at the hands of a spouse. By breaking the vow between husband and wife, our lives seem to be in constant terror as Satan takes over a man or woman and leads them on a destructive pattern that leaves the spouse and family feeling as if they are in a spiritual war zone.

"*I will bring upon you...wasting diseases and fever that will destroy your sight and drain away your life.*" Disease and sickness are ills that can certainly drain us completely of life. And oftentimes disease crops up in our body when our immune system is down. It also has a lot to do with what we put into our body and what is in our environment, such as pollution. The same thing happens in marriage. Men and women ingest or bring issues into the marriage — sex outside the marriage, hatred, anger, resentment, envy, a "single" attitude — that can tear the body of oneness apart. And when those outside ills continuously reside in our marriage, the body of oneness can't take the constant assault. So it tries to fight off the sickness or illness. But it continues to tear down and wear the body out, and eventually, the body succumbs to that disease.

"*You will plant seed in vain, because your enemies will eat it.*" Once we have allowed the sin and the breaking of the covenant to invade the body of oneness, it causes us to give up and quit, which for the marriage means divorce. The thought of divorce is all the seed that the enemy needs to tear your circle of one apart. Once you speak it Satan now knows your thoughts and there will be hell to pay. My first marriage began the turn for the worse when my wife would say things like, "Well, I don't care if we get divorced. At least I'll have my job and my money." I immediately tried to rebuke that statement, asking her not to speak it again because that sets off a domino effect. But the thought prevents us from seeing the beauty of the covenant that we established. Instead, we focus on the negative, which permeates through the body and causes us more harm.

We've got to remind ourselves that we cannot give up in marriage or allow the devil a foothold. How do we prevent it from happening? We feed affirming words to the marriage; we don't take one another for granted; we uphold the covenant to love, honor and respect one another. The moment the body of oneness looks like its immune system is going down, we have to feed it Vitamin C — Christ, feed it some liquids — the freshness of the Holy Spirit, and seek the healing of God.

The reward of the covenant comes out of our obedience. Isaiah 1:19 says, *"If you are willing and obedient, you will eat the best from the land."*

When a man and woman are in complete agreement, respect one another and honor the covenant, they will have the best that marriage has to offer. Everything they do and touch will be blessed and anointed by God. You name it: finances, children, job, family, church, and the union.

I am a living testimony when you live up to the covenant. My wife and I fully understand what we entered into on April 21, 2001. Our aim each day has been to abide by that covenant and allow God to rule over our lives. We trust Him in all that we do and are thankful for whatever He has given us. We don't want for anything. He has given us all that we need. We only seek to avail ourselves to the will of God and where He leads us, we will go, and when He tells us to speak, we do so.

As long as the children of God remember that the marriage covenant will be affirmed to allow our marriages to become living witnesses to others and that when we give God all the glory and follow his precepts, we will reap the blessings He has stored up for us.

I know some of you have not held firm to the covenant at all times. I'm right there with you. But you don't have to sweat last week or yesterday. If your marriage is still intact, albeit barely, that means that God has continued to give you grace and mercy and has not turned His back on you. Yet don't continue on that path. Follow the children of Israel and rededicate yourself to the covenant God made with you and the covenant you and your spouse made with one another. I can guarantee you that when both man and woman

— husband and wife — seek *"ye first the kingdom of God,"* the marriage will be enriched and you will *"eat the best from the land."*

# Marriage: I'm not your momma or daddy

**W**hen a man and woman unite in marriage it is two people who are choosing to spend the rest of their lives with one another. Check that — it's two adults who are making an adult decision to marry.

I emphasize adult because we need to understand that marriage is not for the young at heart or mind. Life is already difficulty for an individual; it is doubly hard when there is more than one person involved. In Eugene Peterson's Bible version, *The Message*, he quotes Jesus in Matthew 19 saying, *"Not everyone is mature enough to live a married life...if you're capable of growing into the largeness of marriage, do it."*

I wish everyone that I have encountered had read that scripture because it is so important.

The Godly husband and the Godly wife must understand that they have left the homes of their parents and are now living as one. No longer can we make mistakes and run to our momma and daddy to bail us out; this time, we must fend for ourselves. That includes a number of areas, including finance, work, communication inside of the marriage and the raising of children.

Recently, I had a number of family members visit our home in Dallas, and we had a chance to sit down and talk with my cousin and his fiancée, (now wife). As we talked about those things couples do that drive us crazy, she began to lament about her fiancée absolutely refuses to put his clothes in the hamper (Yes, they are living together before marriage, but that's another story!). She said no matter how much she tried, he would not do anything about it. It drives her nuts because she hates to see clothes all over the place and his attitude was, "Ain't no big deal, so why bother."

Now, listen bruhs. I know we like to continue as if we are single, but my cousin was absolutely wrong. He should be considerate of her and remember that he does not live alone and shouldn't be so carefree about this matter.

But I told his fiancée that the best way to teach him is to not complain and complain, but to let him drop his clothes all over the bedroom and just sit back and allow that pile of clothes to get larger and larger. Yes, she would be simmering inside, but he had to be taught a lesson. He would eventually run out of clothes and would have to resort to doing something about the mess he created. More likely than not, the brother would catch on that what he is doing doesn't make sense and that he should get his act together. It is also a tactic that my parents used on me as a kid. There was nothing worse than wanting to wear that favorite shirt, only to discover that it was dirty and under a pile of clothes. She also didn't see it was a problem with her leaving glasses and plates all over the house. As I told her, your mess is equal to his mess.

I can hear some wives getting mad because they have experienced the same thing. But I also understand that all the small issues that may drive us nuts are not worth the anxiety, stress, anger and eventual argument with a spouse. Frankly, some stuff just ain't worth the drama. If he or she doesn't straighten out, then that means taking the issue to another level. Living in a dirty environment isn't good. Again, we must respect one another in the process.

Early in my marriage to Jacquie, she washed some shirts and shorts that I normally dry clean. When I saw that these items had shrunk, I was hot! I asked her why in the world would she knowingly wash some items that needed to be dry-cleaned. She responded by saying that she didn't know that was the case. I said that she should have read the tags on the clothes, and she said that nearly all of her clothes were wash and wear and I was the one with all the "special clothes." For a second, there I was about to really go off. But then I said, "Wait a minute. This isn't worth an argument." I then told her that from now on I would sort all of clothes. It wasn't a problem because I also wash clothes in my household and I am used to doing it. She was thankful because that made it easier for her when she washed to have all the clothes sorted.

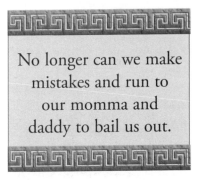

No longer can we make mistakes and run to our momma and daddy to bail us out.

What did I do? I chose not to allow something so small to fester into a larger problem. I just thought of a simple way to resolve the issue and go about my day.

The issue of sorting clothes and leaving stuff all over the house isn't the same. But the commonality is that I refused to allow a small issue to lead to a divisive argument. I rationalized the decision and decided to talk and think my way through it rather than get upset. That's what we should always do: Look at the problem, come up with a compromise and then move on. The point to remember is that we left our momma and daddy at home.

They are not there to do the work that we used to hand off to them. Second, no one wants to hear a man constantly complaining about this or that. Proverbs 19:13 says that "*a foolish son is his father's ruin.*" Of course, it also says that "*a quarrelsome wife is like a constant dripping.*" No man or woman wants to hear someone complain, and if so, we often say, "Don't talk to me like you're my mother or dad." To that person I say, "Stop acting like a child!"

Each husband and wife should always be mindful that they are sharing a living space with another person that they have chosen to love and be with until death do us part. In order to keep harmony within the home, both parties must work to ensure that they are not taking the other for granted.

*Marriage Exercise: Sit down, grab a sheet of paper and jot down all of the little things that your spouse does that drives you crazy. Don't just think about the big-ticket items; be sure to write down all of those small things that irk you beyond belief. Then*

*I want each one of you to exchange lists. Remember, THIS IS NOT AN EXERCISE FOR AN ARGUMENT. Also, don't blow your spouse off by saying some of the stuff on the list is ridiculous. Each of you should make an honest effort to be more attentive to what you do. What is meaningless to you as a wife is important to your husband. If your bad habit is not putting items back in the refrigerator or the kitchen cabinet, make a conscious effort to do so.*

What we want is a happy home that is devoid of drama. Doing this exercise may make you aware of some things that you didn't even believe you were doing. Now that you are aware, make the effort! You may discover that your husband and wife will respond positively to your attentiveness. Lastly, nothing is too small for prayer. Put such issues on your prayer list and pray that God brings a change in the actions of your spouse.

# Marriage: The spiritual covering of a husband

My wife is an ordained minister, but when it comes to leading the prayer at the dinner table or going to God on behalf of a family member in trouble, she looks to me to do so.

She is not weak, meek or lazy; she simply maintains the position that if God has given man dominion over everything on earth, and then I am to assume my role as the priest, provider and protector of the family. Jacquie is extremely comfortable in her role as a pastor, but she also makes it clear that she will not be married to a man who is willing to sit back and let her do all the heavy lifting when it comes to spiritual issues. And I will not be a man who will shirk from that responsibility.

As you peruse through Genesis, God clearly gave Adam the mandate to be ruler over earth (Genesis 1:28). He established the order of the family, and that is for the man to provide the spiritual covering of the husband.

Yet far too many men are running from the role that God has given us. I see countless men — white, black, Asian, Hispanic or any other ethnic group — who are not leading their families spiritually. Their children are running completely out of control, their wives are acting as both father and mother, and all the man can ask is, "What's for dinner?" and where is his beer. This, gentlemen, is not spiritually covering your family.

Men have assumed the position that is the woman's job to deal with the children. But again, God said that man has dominion over all of earth. That even includes the children! No man should sit back and say the job of raising children is the sole province of women. Ephesians 6:3 tell us that fathers should not exasperate their children. "Instead, bring them up in the training and instruction of the Lord."

A father is to instill discipline and guidance in his child. Read scripture and understand that Jesus was a carpenter. How did he learn his trade? By being at the side of his father. That means that fathers today are to have a strong and visible role in the life of the child. But too many of us are distant, choosing to sit back and call on our wives to handle the job.

This is evident when you look at a lot of the commercials on television today. The father comes into the kitchen and upon seeing the child creating a mess, he says, "Where is your mother?" I wanted to kick over the television set after yelling, "Where is the mother? Why can't your sorry behind handle the child?!" Again, we have assumed a hands-off approach to children and that will catch up with us later in the child's life.

**Priest**

It is the absolute duty of the husband to lead his family in prayer and be the example by which the family follows. If your children are wayward and aren't following in the ways of the Lord, it is likely because they didn't see daddy praying, meditating, studying the Word, and applying it to the family's every day life.

When you read scripture, Abraham's wife, Sarah, called him lord. This is not to mean that she saw Abraham as her personal god. It is written as such because Sarah looked to Abraham to be the priest of the family. He was to lead the family and set the example, rather than look to someone else to lead his family.

When my wife is traveling around the country teaching and preaching, I am constantly interceding and praying on her behalf. I want to know what time she will be speaking because at that very moment I want to be in conversation with God so that He may touch her, anoint her and remove any obstacles that may be in her way.

There are times when I have to make a decision about a job or a potential client. She is comfortable in knowing that I am praying to God for guidance in all that I do. By seeing her husband bowing down to the Lord and seeking His direction for my life, she knows that I have the best interests of the family at heart.

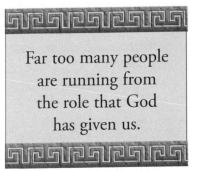

Far too many people are running from the role that God has given us.

Brother, if you know that you are shirking in your responsibility as the priest of your family, make the decision today to put down the remote control or the golf sticks for a season and begin to study the Word of God. I can guarantee you that your family will be enriched beyond your belief as a result of your spiritual discipline and obedience.

## Protector

In my first marriage my wife would often complain that she didn't like it when we would come home and I would insist on opening the door. She was of the feeling that I didn't need to walk in front of her because she felt like she was following behind me, and as an independent woman who made more money than I did, she was very capable of opening the door herself.

She was right. She did make more money than me and was capable of opening the door for herself, but she didn't understand that what I was doing was merely what I had been taught.

As a child, whenever the family returned from an outing, my dad would never allow us to go into the house before him. He would tell the six of us (five children and my mother) to stand on the porch and wait for him before going into the house. You see, my dad took the position that if something evil was behind that door, he would take the brunt of it in order to protect us. If there was a robber in the house, my dad wanted to be the one to confront the robber. He was simply making sure that his family was protected.

I recall in junior high school a few thugs wanted to beat up my brother and myself. It seems that a "Roland" had ticked off the cousin of one of the thugs and they thought it was me, when in fact it was another person by the same name who rode our bus. When my dad got wind of the threats he drove up to the school, got on the bus, and told all 80 students that not a single one of them was to lay a hand on the two of us or they would suffer the consequences of facing him head on. One guy had the audacity to pull a knife on my father. Amused, my dad simply snatched the knife out of the kid's hand and told him never to pull a stunt like that again.

They got the point and we were left alone.

My dad wasn't one to always bail us out of troubling situations. But when his family was potentially harmed, he was willing to put his life on the line.

That, folks, is what happens when the spiritual covering of a husband extends to being a protector.

## Provider

I can't stand a tired, shiftless, trifling man who sits on his behind and doesn't work to provide for his family. If I have to work three jobs to keep my lights on, put food on the table and put clothes on the back of my wife and (future) children, then I will do so.

A husband should financially cover his wife and family. This doesn't mean that he has to put his ego above the family's by insisting that he be the sole breadwinner and "bring home the bacon." But the man must work and provide sustenance for his family.

This doesn't mean that he has to be a stockbroker, doctor, lawyer or some white-collar worker. As long as he is doing a respectable job and holding down his own, I support him 100 percent.

Far too many men and women have gotten stuck in this rut of saying, "He's got to have what I got and he must be on my level." As long as your focus is on the material and not the spiritual, then you will have some screwed up priorities.

If I come across a woman who has her stuff together, doesn't wallow in drama and is willing to be led by the Lord, then I don't care if she doesn't have the education, or the job or the car I have. I know that once my stuff gets with her stuff it all of a sudden becomes our stuff!

Our marriages are crumbling today because men and women are caught up in the game of "stuff." They are more concerned with material possessions and who makes the most. Husbands and wives should keep in mind that marriage is "we-us-our." Leave the "I-my" for single folks!

Lastly, fellas, being the protector doesn't mean that you are to be foolish with the family's finances. I will deal with this issue more when I tackle submission, but if your wife has the gift of money management, investing and solid stewardship, be a strong man of God and recognize her gifts. You don't have to be Mr. Macho and be in control of the checkbook. Remember: she is your partner and your lover. The two of you can work together to build a solid financial life.

When I met Jacquie, I told her that I didn't want to see a bill. She was good at taking care of all that kind of stuff. At that time, with my busy schedule and having to handle work for *Savoy* Magazine, BlackAmericaWeb.com, publishing books and writing a nationally syndicated column, I didn't want to worry about whether I mailed the phone bill. She was cool with that and said, "I got it." When I get my check, I deposit it and she handles all of the other stuff. I'm not naive to not know what's in the bank, but we have a system that works in our household. There is shared responsibility in everything, but she takes the lead in this area.

Marriages should not be ending at the courthouse because of fights over money. Men, we should be providing for the family financially, but let's also protect the peace in the house and not tear ourselves up over financial issues.

*Exercise: I want every man to sit down and truly examine himself and ask, "Am I honestly and truly covering my family spiritually?" It all begins with you. As the husband you must be in right relationship with the Lord in order to lead your family. You can't step out here and lead when you yourself are not allowing God to lead you. If you are saved and committed to Christ, sit down and write out your strengths and weaknesses in the area of family leadership. Then present that list to God and ask Him to guide you and direct you. Second, take baby steps in leading your family. If you've sat back and done nothing for years, it will be culture shock for you to all of a sudden start dropping the hammer. Phase it all in over a period of time, and allow your family to grow in the fullness of God.*

# Marriage: The spiritual undergirding of a wife

**W**henever I have a business meeting, Jacquie always wants to know whom I am meeting with and at what time. She is not trying to be nosy and get in my business. Instead, she wants to be in prayer at the exact time so that God will provide me the proper discernment. I'll do the same thing when she is on the road teaching and preaching; I want to know when she will be speaking so I can intercede on her behalf so that she will be flanked by angels and not have Satan put up roadblocks to prevent her from preaching the Word of God.

Often times many of us enter into agreements, choose to accept jobs or make other decisions based on face value. Yet we often don't consider the other consequences, such as whether we are dealing with ethical individuals or whether the deal is in God's will. I always make sure to apply several biblical principles to every business I'm involved in:

1. Psalms 127:1. "*Unless the Lord builds the house, the builders will labor in vain.*"

2. Psalms 1:1. "*Blessed is the man who does not walk in the counsel of the wicked.*"

3. Proverbs 16:9. "*In his heart a man plans his course, but the Lord determines his steps.*"

I use these verses to help me decide whom I will be involved with business-wise, but I first lean on God for my direction, as well as the discernment and wisdom of my wife.

As a Godly wife, Jacquie clearly understands her role as a *"suitable helper"* for me (Genesis 2:18). She submits to me as the head of the household (Ephesians 5:22) because she knows that I submit to God. She knows and understands that I will not do anything to harm our family and lead us down a negative path. She is completely supportive of what I do and vice versa.

Just as I am a Godly husband who provides the spiritual covering for my family, she is truly an undergirding wife.

Undergirding is not a biblical word but certainly one that applies to God-led marriages. Random House defines the word undergird as "to strengthen; to give fundamental support to; provide with a sound or secure basis." Now I'm a strong man of God who will do anything and everything to support my family. But my wife knows that there are times when my spirit is down and my focus may be off. That's why she is constantly undergirding our family to make sure that we are moving in the right direction. That's what we call a suitable helper.

Just visualize this for a second. If I'm spiritual covering and she is undergirding, that means what is in the middle — the marriage — is completely protected from all sides. There are no cracks and crevices that can cause the foundation to break away. Do you want some scripture to back up my position? Turn to Ephesians 4:15, where Paul writes: *"Instead, speaking the truth in love, we will in all things grow up into him who is the head, that is, Christ. From him the whole body, joined and held together by every supporting ligament, grows and builds itself up in love, as each part does its work."* Both the husband and the wife have responsibilities, even though they are married in oneness. And for that oneness to grow and thrive, we are to do our work and depend on one another for the organism called marriage to expand.

That is a deep concept to many women and men, especially men, who believe in taking everything on their shoulders. "I got it." "I can handle it."

"No, baby, you don't have to worry about a thing." That stuff sounds nice and wonderful, but no woman or man can handle it all. And if they do, I can guarantee you that the stress of having to carry all that weight will weigh them down and ultimately destroy them. A husband and wife are a team that is in this thing together, and they should operate like that at all times. My wife prays for my health, welfare and being. She wants to see my vibrant and strong at all times because I am her husband, lover and partner. If I'm traveling she will ask about my eating habits and whether I'm working out.

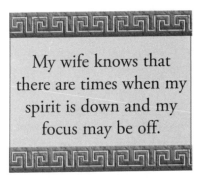

My wife knows that there are times when my spirit is down and my focus may be off.

She will send me messages on my two-way reminding me to eat (I have a habit of going 12 to 14 hours non-stop). She'll send messages of love, prayer and support throughout the day. Trust me, on difficult days, I look forward to my two-way beeping or vibrating!

We also must strive to lose our expectations and pre-determined roles. We must look at one another and ascertain who does what and how we can operate at maximum efficiency for the sake of the marriage.

A lot of my friends laugh when I tell them that my wife typically gets our car serviced, washed or takes the trash out. They think I'm being a slacker for not doing those things, but the two of us tell them as a woman who was single for 36 years (now 40), she was accustomed to doing those things. And as she'll tell you, I'm so consumed with being editor of BlackAmericaWeb.com, news editor of *Savoy* Magazine, preparing a nationally syndicated column and building ROMAR Media Group, I am completely focused on the task at hand. While I'm sleeping at 7 a.m. (after going to be around 3 or 4 a.m.) she usually drops the trash off outside and runs her errands. By the time I awake around 9:30 or 10 a.m., she's taken care of those things and I do what I do. I also shop for food, sort and wash clothes, take care of stuff the dry cleaners and other mundane tasks. The key is that both of us understand that we are in this thing together and we don't trip on what others think a man or woman should be doing. We just automatically do what we do and the other fills in the gaps in order for our home to run efficiently.

And I'll be honest, I'm thankful that God has given me a woman who can do some of these things. While recently returning from a trip, we were leaving the airport and my wife turned down the radio and said, "There is a nail in the tire."

"What?" I replied.

"A nail," she said. Now I had no clue that she knew a nail was in the tire, and lo and behold, we pulled into a gas station and there was a nail in the tire.

If left to my devices, I would have driven that car until the tire fell off because I'm oblivious to those things. My mind is normally in so many other places that I don't even think of that unless I see the tire deflated!

I have a friend who is the same way. Michael Williams won't fix a thing. But his wife, Donna? She's known to get under the car at the dealership to show the mechanics what the problem is. For Michael and Donna, that works for them and for Jacquie and I, it works just fine.

We constantly work at helping one another in all that we do, and I'm appreciative of having that undergirding wife. A lot of men have no clue how powerful it is to have a woman spiritually undergirding her husband and family. To do so, that requires a wife to have her face planted in the Word, constantly praying and meditating.

Ever heard of a wife's intuition? I'm convinced that was something God put into a woman because he knew a man would be oblivious to certain things. Remember what I said about my wife praying for me when it comes to business meetings? My sister is a master at that, and it took her husband a long time to figure out that he had better listen to her.

He would often conduct meetings, and on paper, the deal looked solid. But when he would tell her she would say that he shouldn't go into business with the person. His focus was on the money but her spirit said pay attention to the spirit of the person you are doing business with. After entering into several deals that looked great but ultimately failed, he finally recognized her gift — she was trying to be a "helper" — and began to run all of his business dealings by her. That ticked some of his associates off who felt that his wife was "meddling" and should "know her place." He quickly figured out that her place was right there with him in the office. I'm convinced that had he first recognized that she was trying to undergird him, he would not have made the business mistakes and suffered from them.

Any woman who is married must always have her man's back. I'll use this illustration. We often times think of oneness as looking like a man and wife embracing, thereby preventing anyone from coming between them. To me, that sounds like oneness. But I also view oneness as a husband and wife standing with their backs to one another, constantly looking out for distractions and dangers that could target their spouse. By standing back-to-back, they are protecting each other from whatever may come their way.

That's how we should also look at spiritual undergirding. A woman is supporting the marriage and family through her prayers, which allows the husband and children to be all that they can be.

*Exercise: Many of you may not be a husband who spiritually covers his family. You also may not be a wife who spiritually undergirds her mate. But beginning today, you can begin to do just that. All it takes is you taking the initial step. It doesn't have to be something grand and accompanied by lots of fanfare. When your spouse is in bed sleep, lay your hands on their head, chest and stomach and pray to God to anoint them and touch them. Stop the bickering and infighting and find common ground in your household. Learn to keep unnecessary things from cluttering his mind, and the same goes for the wife. When the husband and wife are allowed to think clearly, the two of you will grow and thrive.*

*You can gently ask your husband when is he meeting with his boss about his evaluation or when the kids are taking a test at school, and begin to pray for them before the meeting and test and during the meeting and test. You may quickly discover that not only will God envelope you with his Holy Spirit, but also touch and anoint your husband and family, so they can be the best that God wants them to be.*

*Also, carefully study all of Ephesians, especially chapters 4 and 5. And be sure to pick up your copy of The Power of a Praying Wife; The Power of a Praying Husband; and The Power of a Praying Parent by Stormie Omartian.*

# Marriage: Submission, oh, what a beautiful thing!

If you are looking for a guaranteed argument from a woman, just bring up the topic of submission. The nostrils will flare out, the ears will get perky, their back will get rigid, and then it's on!

At a book signing several years ago for Michael Eric Dyson, I had a chance to talk to his wife, Marcia, and the topic of submission came up. Marcia, who, like her husband, is an ordained minister, shot me a look of contempt and said, "Oh, no! Don't bring up that submission junk!" I quickly calmed her down, clearly seeing that the topic wasn't at the top of her discussion list. I gently took her hand and lead her to the bookshelf to find P.B. Wilson's *Liberated Through Submission: God's Design for Freedom in All Relationships*. I asked Marcia to pick up Wilson's book and give me a call so we can discuss her thoughts on it. I'm still waiting for the call.

It is the same reaction that countless other women have heard when the dreaded word comes up. Yes, a feeling of dread and anger is the typical response. This 10-letter word has started heated dialogues and even led some folks to fight one another. But much of this is due to individuals using a worldly definition for a spiritual act; using submission as a negative rather than a positive word; and a complete failure to understand the biblical reasons and justifications for submission. That is the case because so many individuals in the church, namely men, have chosen to harp on Scripture where it says that a woman is to submit to a man as head, and that she can't speak in church (1 Corinthians 14:34) and must learn in quiet and *"full submission"* (1 Timothy 2:11). Yes, that is certainly what Scripture says, but that is only a small part of the story of submission. The issue has gotten so contentious that my pastor in Dallas, the Rev. Frederick D. Haynes, III has even stopped using the part of submission when he performs marriage ceremonies because so many folks have absolutely no clue to its biblical meaning.

This essay may not change your opinion of submission. But that is not my mission. It is simply to share with you what God has shared and deposited in me about submission and how it can relax your fears, revive your spirit, and reinvigorate your marriage.

Out of all the Scriptures that deal with submission, the one that is often cited is Ephesians 5:22-24: *"Wives, submit to your husbands as to the Lord. For the husband is the head of the wife as Christ is the head of the church, his body, of which he is the Savior. Now as the church submits to Christ, so also wives should submit to their husbands in everything."* For those who freak out with regards to this issue, let's be clear that when Scripture refers to submission it does not have the same definition as the world, which often views it as "the state of being submissive; acknowledgement of inferiority or dependence; humble or suppliant behavior; meekness; resignation."

Scripture is not telling women to shut up, be quiet, not have an opinion, and do whatever her husband says. The act of biblical submission means an individual — man or woman — has to first create such a relationship with the Lord that he or she first submits their all to Christ. Before you can submit yourself to your mate, you must first be in submission to Christ. Jesus serves as our example in this by virtue of his own submission to God. In Hebrews 5:7, it is written: *"During the days of Jesus' life on earth, and petitions with loud cries and tears to the one who could save him from death, and he was heard because of his reverent submission."* Jesus clearly understood the direction that God was giving him, therefore, he chose to operate in God's will and submit to that will. By virtue of Jesus submitting, or yielding power and authority to God over his life, his prayers were heard by God. Within the context of marriage, a wife must first have a relationship with Christ so that she understands what is required of a wife. When that wife has that relationship, she then must be sure that she is marrying an individual that also operates within the will of God. If not, then she will be submitting, or yielding authority to a power that is not what God has ordained, thus there will be chaos in the marriage.

My wife has no problem submitting within our marriage because she fully knows that I don't do anything in our marriage without first seeking God's direction. If God says yes, we do it. If God says no, we don't do it, despite anything that my human self may choose to say or do. Obedience is the key in this. More importantly, I fully understand that my wife has been specially designed because Genesis 2:18 says, *"It is not good for the man to be alone. I will make a helper suitable for him."* Eugene Peterson's *The Message* says, *"I'll make him a helper, a companion."*

As a man of God, I must acknowledge that I don't know it all. That's why God has provided me a mate with skills and talents that are to enhance the marriage and provide fulfillment. This then mandates that I fully trust and respect the gifts of my wife and know that she isn't doing anything that is meant to hurt or harm the marriage or me. Some of you are scratching your heads and saying, *"But if the man is the head, and he says we are going to do something, what role does the wife have in it?"*

I'm glad you asked. If God has equipped your wife with the skills of money management and finance, why in the world would you choose to make financial decisions in the marriage without her input? Better yet, let her handle that!

She's the expert-not you-so yield to her skill set! God has clearly designed the woman to "help" her mate and it's silly to ignore the wealth of information sitting in front of you!

A man must not seek his own counsel in these areas, but instead, he must submit himself to God and all that God has designed. Are you looking for some Scripture to back that up? Cool, go to Ephesians 5:21, where it says, *"Submit to one another out of reverence for Christ."* We are not asked to simply submit to someone else and that's it. We are all asked to submit to one another out of reverence for Christ. That means that we are to love, honor and respect one another. Men, we are to love our wives, honor our wives, AND respect the gifts and talents they have. If we don't, and choose to go our own way, then we are not truly submitting to God because we are ignoring the blessings that he has placed in our lives to assist in decision-making.

No man can ever expect his wife to lovingly submit to him if he doesn't have a relationship with Christ. That man can't hold up Scripture and say, "Gotcha!" if he isn't himself submitting to the will of God. If God is telling you one thing and you are doing another, then why in the world do you think a woman will feel comfortable submitting to you? That man must first submit to God before he can ever expect his wife to submit to him. And I strongly believe that's one of the reasons why so many women are angry at submission. They have seen countless men not do this but try to use Scripture against them. Sorry, bruhs! YOU must be a shining example in this area. Your wife needs to see you praying, reading Scripture and following God's will for your life before she will have the complete confidence that you have her best interest at heart. If she sees such an act of submission on your part, then she will gladly submit.

But this isn't just me talking. Ephesians 5:25 mandates that "*husbands, love your wives, just as Christ loved the church and gave himself up for her to make her holy, cleansing her by the washing with water through the word, and to present her to himself as a radiant church, without stain or wrinkle or any other blemish, but holy and blameless.*" Fellas, you must heed this word! By bringing a full act of submission on your part, you will render yourself without stain and operate in a constant state of holiness. Once that is done, then your wife can't help but submit to you because you are taking directions directly from the Master. If Jesus Christ wasn't obedient to God and didn't submit to His will, do you think any of us would be here today following his every commandment? No! So it's time for us to put our worldly thoughts away and begin to operate within the kingdom as men and women of God who are more than willing to submit.

I am convinced that if you are having trouble submitting to your husband or wife, you have yet to submit your life to Christ. Let me repeat that: I didn't say 25% or 50% or 75% or 98%; you are called to completely turn yourself over so that God will guide your life accordingly. God garners that kind of trust because He has a track record of not leading you astray. So if your husband has that same kind of track record, then you must be willing to operate in full submission because he has your best interests at heart and won't lead you astray.

You may say that you have tried to do that but your husband won't cooperate. Bruh, you may argue that you submit to God's will but your wife is hell bent on doing her own thing. If this is the case, then you must be honest with yourself and ask if this is the woman God set aside for you. If so, the two of you must come to an understanding as to where you stand with God as an individual and as a couple. As long as the two of you have a different view of faith within your life and that of your marriage, you are bound to have countless problems.

I can honestly say that I wish I had a better grasp on submission in my teenage years. Once I understood that I, Roland Sebastian Martin, am to fully and completely turn my life over to Christ and submit to His will, then my life was on the proper path. And if that is done in life, and the same attitude is taken into our marriages, then we will surely have loving and drama-free marriages that will glorify God and be just what we always imagined them to be.

*Exercise: Sit down and ask yourself if you are submitting your life to God. Do you seek God's wisdom before making any decision? Are you aware of your gifts and how God wants you to use them? Do you fully know what your weaknesses are and how to recognize them in the future? After answering those questions, then begin to incorporate the concept of submission into every decision you make. I'm confident you will then begin to see how beautiful it can be within your life, and then your marriage.*

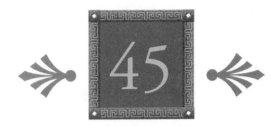

# Marriage: 'Honey, I forgive you'

"I forgive you" could probably the three hardest words for a lot of us to say. No matter how large our Bible is and how many days we go to church a week, having to ask, offer, seek or accept forgiveness is incredibly difficult for humans to do. This human frailty we possess could have a lot to do with the personal pain we suffer when someone has wronged us or let us down. Our anger, resentment and frustration often comes out of us in such situations and we don't want to let go of those feelings because we so desperately want to carry that grudge around. Yet we can't, especially when God tells us that we shouldn't.

Look, I'm not going to be carefree and pass over the hurt and pain someone may feel as a result of a spouse cheating on them. It would be ridiculous to not express the pain a parent feels when their teenage child comes home and says that they are expecting or have fathered a child. If a friend has forgotten our birthday or special occasion, we react with sadness or anger because we feel we have been taken for granted. Many of these scenarios are common within marriage because it is such a close relationship, and one that is ripe for events that will require forgiveness.

Yet despite the intense pain and suffering we endure because of any number of actions, there is no feeling that can be compared to that of forgiveness. It is undoubtedly the most unselfish and liberating thing that any of us could do for others and ourselves. That may come as a shock to some, but it's true. When we are mature enough to look someone in the eye who has hurt us and actually say with full confidence and sincerity, "I forgive you," then we have achieved a significant milestone as a Christian. Better yet, we have moved closer to living in the image of Christ.

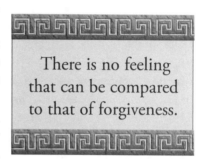

There is no feeling that can be compared to that of forgiveness.

If you do a word search of the word forgive in the Bible (try www.Biblegateway.com), you will find 117 references. There are plenty that have to do with God not forgiving His children for turning their back on him, yet you will find more examples of sins being forgiven than anything else.

Despite the wretched actions by the children of Israel in celebrating false gods, even after God freed them from Egypt, God still managed to forgive them. Joseph was asked to forgive his brothers after they, in a fit of jealously, threw him into the grave and left him for dead. Committing an act of jealousy or hatred against us is cruel and goes against everything that we stand for in the faith. But the extension of grace and mercy clearly supercedes that.

Just take a moment and think back to all of the sins you have committed. Isn't it amazing that you were allowed to keep living and that God continue to bless you, despite all of the stuff you did? So if God was big enough to forgive us for our sins, why should we continue to hold contempt for our wife or husband, who has committed a sin, pledged to repent and has gotten on the road to recovery?

By them offering all of that and for us to continue to not grant forgiveness makes us hypocritical Christians. Life has its ups and downs and there will be times when you feel as if you have been wronged by your response. The burden of carrying around unforgiven issues is far too much for any individual to bear. We must release all of that pain to God. If He has forgiven our transgressions, why do you continue to harbor them? I expect to get more emails saying, "You just don't understand." "He hurt me so much." "I can't trust her again." Again, can God say the same about you? We must all begin to practice forgiveness if we want to move on and live a more fulfilling life.

Now is the time for each and every person to dig deep within their spirit and become like God in extending grace and mercy. Our marriages will be better for it.

*Exercise: Write down the issues you continue to carry around that you haven't forgiven your spouse for. Once you have done that, then resolve within your spirit that you are willing to extend them grace and mercy and forgive them for their transgressions. After that, leave what's in the past in the past.*

# Knowing God's vision for your life I

*Text focus: Habakkuk 2:1-4*

***

"Why am I here?" It is probably one of the most simple, and at the same time, the most profound question many of us could ask ourselves. Many of us go through this life wondering what we are supposed to be doing. Often times we engage in tasks that seem menial and don't have any sort of rhyme or reason to them.

You aren't alone if you have ever asked that question. I've been right there with you. Like many of you, I've gone to church on a consistent basis, read the Word of God and tried to be the best Christian I could be, but there have been moments in my life that I asked that crucial question. Fortunately, the answer began to form in my spirit some 24 years ago, and it has only gotten stronger and more consistent.

But there are many out there who are adults approaching the age of 40, 50 or even 60, and they are still asking the question that seems to have no answer. Look at the photo that accompanies this piece. Imagine a road that doesn't seem to be leading in one direction. We see the yellow stripe, which separates the road: one lane is going in one direction and the other in the opposite direction. The road seems to stretch for miles and miles, as if it is running right into the clouds.

In many ways that describes our situation. We are traveling on a road that sometimes feels as if there isn't a compass in the world that can right us.

Consider an email I received that highlights this difficult issue:

"Brother Roland, awesome articles; very anointed. But I am looking for an article that talks about what a wife can do (in the natural...I know spiritually I must pray) when her husband does not know his purpose or have a vision/mission for his life. Also, the wife has (to) double....so it's hard for her to sit and wait for her husband to 'find himself.' The family is at a stand still; the wife feels frustrated because she is filled with so much creativity and vision; she wants her husband to join her in the journey for their lives. What (do you) think? I've bought him every book on the market about purpose, vision, mission etc. He prays but says he still doesn't know. He went through a business failure a couple of years ago that took some of the wind out of him. He's been floundering ever since. I've been floundering with him....Submission means to be "under the mission" of the head (man)....right now our ship is out a sea without any steering. I feel like taking the wheel!"

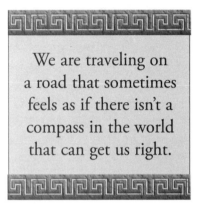

We are traveling on a road that sometimes feels as if there isn't a compass in the world that can get us right.

I was thankful for this sister's email because it takes a bold and courageous person to step out and ask for guidance when faced with such a daunting task. It was also well received because it was a kick in the pants for me to keep writing this column; I got myself caught up in a lot of other work, when I was supposed to have written a series of pieces on vision.

The problem the brother in the email faces is just like what so many of us are going through. We have starts and stops, and it seems like we are going nowhere fast. But what we must realize is that just like when our car is breaking down on us, we need to pull to the side of the road to see what the problem is. Other times we need to call for help when our cursory look under the hood doesn't reveal anything. Then again, we might have to have a lot of work done to fix the problem. And when it gets too bad, we just have to get a whole new car because it would cost too much to fix it.

Our goal is to begin to understand God's vision for our lives, and then for us to begin to act on the vision he has given us.

# Knowing God's vision for your life: Patience

In the piece In Chapter 36, "In Due Time," I told the story of what happened to me in the summer of 1999. For nearly two weeks I would awaken to a voice saying, "Patience." I was going nuts hearing this word because, first, I'm not a morning person, and waking up at 5:30 a.m. wasn't my cup of tea. It also annoyed me because it is one of the virtues that I'm not too fond of! Yet when it comes to the vision that God has for our lives, it is so critical that we understand patience. It is one of the hallmarks of our Christian faith because everything has to happen at the right time and in the right season.

Pick up your Bible and re-read the gospels of Matthew, Mark, Luke and John. One of the more consistent items we will read is Jesus constantly telling His followers and those who He healed not to tell who He was. Although from the moment He was born Jesus knew what His purpose in life was, it required Him to be silent until it was the right time to say who He was, which was the triumphal entry described in Matthew 21.

In Matthew 8, Jesus cured the man with leprosy and told him (v. 4): "*See that you don't tell anyone.*" He even politely scolded his mother for potentially revealing who he was in John 2, at the wedding feast where they run out of wine. After telling him about the problem, Jesus tells his mother, *"Dear, woman, why do you involve me? My time has not yet come."* Again, He didn't want to show His power until it was time for the son of God to be revealed.

We must fall under the same rules when it applies to the vision that God has for us. When it is time for that vision to be unveiled to our family, friends and associates, then we are to do so. But that requires extreme patience on our part.

I will be the first to admit that that is extremely hard and tempting.

In July 2000, I was instructed by God to write down the vision that He gave me for my future career path. I had already eclipsed all of my life's goals by the age of 30, but remember, that was with my small thinking. God had a much greater plan to use me for His glory. I thought it would take me a lifetime to work as a news director/morning anchor at a radio station; managing editor of two newspapers; cover a national political convention; produce a TV show for a television network; and cover a host of major news stories and newsmakers.

But by the age of 29 I had already done all of that and it was time to set new goals. Yet this time, it would not be at my own choosing; it was God's agenda that I would be operating from.

So I commenced to write down all that he had me do, which included a full-scale media company that would include owning newspapers, television and radio programming, books, speaking engagements and a host of other exciting ventures. Once I finished, God then said, "Now put it on the shelf."

"Say what?!" At the time I was not working fulltime and was struggling mightily with my finances. And here I had sat down and written an extensive document that outlined all sorts of wonderful plans. I was ready to conquer the world, but God quickly reminded me that it was He who was in charge of this plan.

I didn't quite understand why I had to wait on the Lord to put the plan into action so I took my issues straight to Him. He said, "Roland, there are some individuals and some things that I must put in place before much of this can take place. You must wait until I tell you it is time to move before you can do any of this."

I'll be honest; I was hurt and had no clue as to what was going on. But God had to show me that while the vision I was given was a good one that would come to fruition, it wasn't going to take place tomorrow. I had to put my trust completely in him for it to come about.

Everything has to happen at the right time and in the right season.

Habakkuk 2:1-4 contains several instructions, including: *"the revelation awaits an appointed time"*; *"it will not prove false"*; and *"though it will linger, wait for it; it will certainly come and will not delay."*

Some of you may be in the same situation I was in. You have been given a wonderful vision for your family, children, career and/or ministry, and you're wondering why nothing has happened. Don't fret! A lot is happening that you aren't aware of.

I soon learned that as the months passed by I was coming across individuals who would have a profound impact on the vision that God had given me. I had been blessed to meet wonderful financial minds that would advise me on how to set up my business. There were people in television ministry who would come into my life, and we would strike up a friendship that would pave the way for some of the television concepts I had to get placed on the air (none have been done so far, but it will happen in the near future). It was great to meet potential investors who could finance the company that God had entrusted to me.

There are three critical issues to remember about God's vision for your life:

1. *"Let God and get out of the way."* Nothing operates on your timetable; when God says it's time, it's time. Remember what Jesus told his mother, "My time has not yet come!" The time may not have come for the vision that you have been given to be put into place. Bishop T.D. Jakes may have been given the vision he is now implementing a long time ago when he was a country preacher in West Virginia, but years had to go by and

lessons had to be learned before many aspects of his ministry were put into action. Again, he had to have the patience to wait on God to arrange the necessary pieces and people in order for that vision to come to fruition.

2. **Continue to work when it looks like nothing is getting done.** A part of waiting on God is to remain faithful, even when you can't see the blessings taking place. We are a society that likes to see stuff happening. Far too many of us can't sit back and know that things are being taken care of. We want to make a phone call or have someone check on whether what is supposed to be done gets done. But we can't do that with God. We must have the faith and patience know that if God said it was going to happen, that's the end of the conversation. But by no means stop working! At no time did I stop learning about finance, how to publish books, what equipment is required to produce a television show and all the necessary ingredients to making my media company go from something on paper to fruition. I had to go out and do the hard work that is required. God will do his part, but Roland had to do his part. God gives us the vision, but we are to follow it and put it into place. If not, we aren't holding up our end of the bargain.

3. **Don't outrun the vision.** A lot of us like to move faster than what we are supposed to do. If God has said that we are going to be doing X, Y and Z in five years, why do we insist on trying to make it happen tomorrow? Remember, the seed is planted now so it can begin to grow, but we can't reap any fruit from that tree until it is ready to produce a harvest. We must always allow God to lead us, and when it is due time for us to do something, than so be it. The Lord has blessed me with several ideas that will be turned into Christian-based movies, but I'm not to stop what I'm doing and begin writing those scripts today! The

idea has been placed in me and I am to slowly water those ideas, and by year five of my company, put it into action. The same goes for what you may be experiencing. You may have been given an idea, but it's not always supposed to happen today. Listen to God speak to your spirit as to when that idea is to grow and bloom.

Remember, he told Nehemiah to rebuild the wall of Jerusalem, but it took some time for it to happen. None of God's visions are fulfilled overnight!

*Exercise: Begin to list God's vision for you, and open your spirit to receive his direction for your life. Listen intently as to when different parts of the vision are supposed to be put into action. And immediately write them down. The key to developing patience in this area of your life is to have the proper spiritual discernment.*

# Rediscovering
# the "C" in YWCA

Six months after being hired as CEO of the nation's first women's organization, Patricia Ireland was effectively told to gather up her brand of advocacy and take a hike.

Her firing was about as stunning as her hiring by the National Coordinating Board of the Young Women's Christian Association.

From the moment she was named to the post, Christian organizations vehemently protested the decision, stating that the former leader of the National Organization of Women was unfit to lead the YWCA because of her fierce pro-choice views. They also didn't like the fact that during her tenure at NOW, the married Ireland lived with a woman in Washington, D.C., suggesting that she was a lesbian (Ireland has steadfastly refused to discuss her sexuality). And when she asked when she was hired whether she was a Christian, Ireland skated around the issue.

YWCA leaders tried to suggest that the faith-based complaints about Ireland didn't play a role in their decision. "We have the deepest admiration for Ms. Ireland's dedication to women's issues and social justice, but the YWCA has proved to be the wrong platform for her to advocate for these issues," said NCB Chairman Audrey Peeples in a news release.

That is about as a disingenuous statement as anyone can come up with.

YWCA officials tried to dance all around the issue, but the real problem with Ireland's hiring and firing was that it shows the YWCA was an organization that is absolutely clueless as to what its purpose is.

In the press release announcing Ireland's firing, this is how the YWCA described itself: "For more than 150 years, the YWCA has been pioneering programs and services for communities across the country. The organization provides shelters for women and families, administers violence prevention programs for more than 700,000 women and children, and serves more than 750,000 children in child care and after-school programs. The organization is continuing its commitment to its historic, grassroots drive to address the issues facing women and girls and eliminate racism."

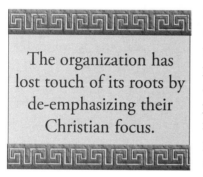

The organization has lost touch of its roots by de-emphasizing their Christian focus.

Yet on its website describing the YWCA's history, it says that "the programs, and the locations have changed many times over the years, but the basic purpose of the YWCA has not."

In fact, the YWCA has changed. They rarely ever refer to themselves as the Young Women's Christian Association, choosing to use their acronym in a clear attempt to avoid mentioning the "C" word. This is a long way from an organization that grew out of prayer groups established in Great Britain during the mid-19th century. The influence of the group gravitated to America, and the various groups of the Ladies Christian Organization eventually rallied together and formed the Young Women's Christian Association, which served to provide opportunities for young women with a non-denominational but spiritual focus.

Like it not, the YWCA's Christian values have played a huge role in its success since 1858. But clearly the organization has lost touch of its roots by de-emphasizing their Christian focus. Ask any organization leader and they'll tell you that the moment a group strays from its mission it quickly loses focus and relevance.

Just imagine the Anti-Defamation League not fighting anti-Semitism or the NAACP not really focusing on the needs of African Americans.

There is absolutely nothing wrong with an organization proudly proclaiming its Christian heritage and promoting its ideals to pursue changes in our society. Just look at the Young Men's Christian Association (YMCA), which maintains as its mission: "To put Christian principles into practice through programs that build healthy spirit, mind and body for all."

Now its time for the donors, supporters and leaders of the 326 YWCA associations nationwide to reach down in the depths of their soul to restore the group to its true purpose and mission. If not, they will remain like the children of biblical Israel — wandering in the wilderness because of their disobedience.

Talk to any corporate executive, politician or even men and women of the cloth, and the buzzword today is mentoring. Leaders are besieged every day with e-mails, phone calls and letters from young men and women who seek to have an experienced hand take them under their wing to show them the ropes.

I am a fierce believer in the mentor system, serving in that capacity for a number of aspiring journalists across the country. It has always been my belief that the next generation should be properly prepared and trained in order to carry on the mission of the media.

My wife, Jacquie, has a litany of young women at our church in Houston and across the country who she counsels and mentors, raising them up to know and understand what their role is as women in the kingdom of God.

# Spiritual mentorship

***Text focus: 1 and 2 Kings***

***

Roy Johnson, a dear friend of mine, is one of those folks who are always being hit up to serve as someone's mentor. In fact, Roy — a former assistant managing editor at Sports Illustrated and now editor-in-chief of Men's Fitness — tries not to give his card out because he knows he will be deluged by folks who would love to pick his brain, use him as a reference or try to ride his knowledge and experience into a job in the media world. Please, understand, Roy is appreciative of the eager beavers who reach out to him, but he is quick to say that most people have it all wrong: mentees are supposed to be chosen, and not the other way around.

Some would argue that Roy is wrong in his assessment, but in reality, all he is doing is following the example that God has provided for us.

In 1 Kings 19:14, Elijah was worried and scared to death. He was just coming off of his greatest victory when he defeated Baal's prophets on Mount Carmel, but he was forced to flee after Ahab's wife, Jezreel, ordered his death.

After crying out to the Lord, Elijah said that he had worked feverishly for Him, but the Israelites rejected God's covenant and *"put your prophets to death with the sword. I am the only one left, and now they are trying to kill me too."*

# Spiritual mentorship

God was already taking care of Elijah and protecting him (remember the feeding by the ravens?), but He wanted to make sure Elijah could stop worrying. That's when He commanded Elijah (1 Kings 19:15) to anoint Elisha to succeed him as prophet.

Often times we tell those being mentored that they are lucky for getting the opportunity to sit at the feet of someone with stature, yet we often overlook the fact that the mentor should be a person of accountability and integrity. God knew Elijah's heart. Surely He would not have entrusted him to carry on His work, and then pass that knowledge on, if he wasn't a person of accountability.

Just because a person has a title doesn't mean that they are destined to be a mentor. Remember, Elijah was a prophet of God; there were other prophets. In 1 Kings 18 we see the prophets of Baal. They were not the kind of prophets that we would want to follow and trust because Baal was a little "g" God. They had no standing because their trust and faith wasn't with the Creator.

In order to be someone's spiritual mentor, you really need to be an individual who lives for the Lord and is willing to put all of your trust and faith into Him.

About 11 years ago I was a city hall reporter in Fort Worth, and a seasoned journalist decided to declare himself my mentor. I didn't seek him out but he chose me. When I left the *Austin American-Statesman* to go to the *Fort Worth Star-Telegram*, I commuted back and forth between Austin and Fort Worth. One weekend, this journalist invited me over to dinner to discuss something urgent with me. When I arrived and we sat down to eat, he proceeded to tell me that he had been hearing things from others in Fort Worth and that I was too aggressive and wore my ambition on my sleeve. His words were, "you're a hot dog." I patiently listened, and when he finished, I told him the real deal. I asked him if he had known about the countless times I had availed myself to assist other reporters and to contribute story ideas to the city desk. He said "no." I asked him was he aware that others were making statements about me being an editor and publisher one day because of the promise I showed. He said "no." I asked him if he was aware that the plan was to eventually put me on a management track. He said "no." In essence, this "mentor" had no real knowledge about me or what I did. Folks, that not the kind of mentor I want. I have no problem with anyone advising you or instructing you on how to succeed in life. But when a young journalist's spirit, zeal and zest for life are being squashed by the gossip of jealous journalists, and supposed mentor believes it, that's not the kind of person I want leading me. After that conversation we had very little contact and he never again advised me on anything with my career. I strongly believe that he knew that the sources he cited led him down the wrong path and he chose to put a potential mentor-mentee relationship on the line as a result. Again, everybody isn't destined to be your mentor.

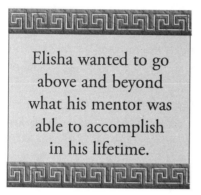

Elisha wanted to go above and beyond what his mentor was able to accomplish in his lifetime.

Keep in mind that Elijah anointed Elisha, but it was Elisha's responsibility to then serve as an understudy of Elijah. He was to listen to his wisdom, learn at his feet and soak up the knowledge that Elijah offered in order to be an effective prophet.

I recall interviewing Barbara Jordan the day Thurgood Marshall died in 1992 for a story in the *Austin American-Statesman* and she talked of visiting him in the 1970s and literally sitting at his feet to listen as this icon of law and justice shared his knowledge with her and others. This is Barbara Jordan, the first black woman elected to Congress from the South since Reconstruction, talking about sitting at the feet of Thurgood Marshall — the legendary Supreme Court Justice Thurgood Marshall, the first African American on the High Court. If Barbara Jordan could recognize the inherent value of that experience, why can't we take the time to do it ourselves? There are some of us in the faith who have come to the conclusion that they have been "anointed" to preach and teach, and don't see the need for further study. It's nice to be blessed with God-given talents and abilities, but those must be honed and refined. There isn't a need to be cocky or arrogant with the position of authority God has given you. Elisha could have stuck out his chest and said, "I'm a prophet." But in essence, he was a baby prophet who needed to learn from his earthly master — Elijah.

I recall the story of a 20-something man who was looking to start a magazine in New York. And his mentor told him to call my friend Roy Johnson. This young whippersnapper called him and said, "I was told to call you but I don't know why I'm calling you because I don't see what value you are bringing to the table." Being a God-fearing man, Roy didn't cuss him out or hang up in his face; he simply finessed himself out of the conversation. Folks, that's not how you treat someone who has knowledge to offer you.

We are to learn from our mentors while they are here because there will come a day when we can't get them on the phone; they can't access their email; they are tied up in meetings or on vacation. And if we're not paying attention while they were teaching us, then we would not be able to deal with our present predicament.

**You've got to make an investment**

Elisha knew that in order be a prophet-in-training, he would have to put all of his time and energy into his new job. At the time of his anointing, Elisha was plowing *"twelve yoke of oxen"* (1 Kings 19:19). When Elijah threw his cloak around him — today we may throw our arms around someone in public to show they are now our understudy — Elisha kissed his parents, disposed of his farming equipment, and followed after Elijah. He knew that the job was so big that he couldn't afford to not be at his side.

If you are willing to sit under the spiritual teaching of someone, you must focus your energies on giving him or her your time and attention. This doesn't necessarily mean leave your job (unless the Lord directs you to do so), but it does mean that making a half-hearted effort will not suffice. Elijah needed all of Elisha's attention if he was going to teach him what he needed to know.

Elisha's devotion to Elijah is seen in 2 Kings 2. Elijah was about to go to heaven and wanted to separate himself from Elisha, but his young prophet made it clear: he wasn't going anywhere. In fact, he told Elijah this on three separate occasions (2:2, 4, 6). That's the kind of devotion that any mentor wants to see, as well as our Lord. He wants to know that we will not forsake Him and will keep our eyes focused on doing His will in our lives.

### Advance the cause

It's incumbent for all of us to understand that the lessons being passed from a mentor on down isn't solely for the purpose of providing knowledge. It is truly about building upon what God has already done.

Bishop Eddie L. Long exemplifies someone who understands the Elijah-Elisha principle.

In his book, *Taking Over,* Long writes that God led him to select his replacement when he was just a young man (Keep in mind that Long was a relatively young pastor in his mid-30s when he made this decision. There are many pastors who wouldn't dare choose their successor, which is one of the reasons why so many ministries die when the founding pastor/leader dies. They didn't follow the example of Elijah or Moses and Joshua).

This young man was teaching a teenage Bible study when Long was walking down the hall. He heard him teach and was instantly taken by him.

Long encouraged him to get his theological training, and when finished, ordained him. They developed a close friendship, and upon seeing his devotion to God and then hearing the Lord's commandment, Long named Curney as his successor.

Like Elijah, Long understood that the vision God gave him must continue beyond his death. Yet Long's replacement, Rev. Jesse Curney III, also must be willing to take the ministry to heights even Long can't envision.

Elisha understood that. In 2 Kings 2:9, Elijah asks his attendant what can be done before he goes to heaven.

*"Let me inherit a double portion of your spirit,"* Elisha replied.

Knowing full well his power, Elijah conceded that was difficult, but assured Elisha that if he was present when he went to heaven, his request would be granted.

# Spiritual mentorship

The Lord told me that Elisha wanted to go above and beyond what his mentor was able to accomplish in his lifetime. As a mentor, we should want to see our mentees rise to new heights and to double what we have done. And if we have trained our mentees appropriately, they will continue that for the next generation and the next generation and the next generation and the next generation.

As a spiritual mentor, it is of no concern what the person you are training will do. If they earn more money, preach to larger crowds, sell more books, witness to more people, so what?! You were charged with assisting them to grow in their faith and that's all God wants you to do. However he chooses to bless them is between them and God.

Yet too many of us are unwilling to mentor someone else because we fear the blessings they may receive. The kingdom of God cannot and will not grow unless we push the next generation to maximize their opportunities and potential to do more, learn more and get better.

I am truly amazed to hear pastors of small churches complain about the explosion of mega-churches. Instead of focusing on the fact that a church is ministering to thousands upon thousands of people, all they are concerned about is the book sales and TV time another minister is getting. Maybe that mega-church pastor asked his or her mentor for a double portion of their blessing!

## Be in position

God and Elijah blessed Elisha tremendously because he wasn't off fooling around and not taking care of his business. He received that double portion because he never left the side of Elijah.

Jerry Rice is the greatest wide receiver in NFL history because when he ran patterns, Steve Young or Joe Montana could throw a ball to a spot and not worry about it because Jerry would be in position to catch it. Rice was always on his game and knew his plays and could read the defense accordingly and adjust his route because he knew the quarterback was doing the same. Rice couldn't do any of that unless he practiced hard during the week, conditioned his body for the game, as well as spent long hours in the video room watching tape. Jerry was prepared for the game, which meant he was prepared to catch the ball. Why was he so successful? Because he was always in position.

When the chariots and horse of fire came to take Elijah home to be with God, guess where Elisha was? Right there. Much like Elisha, we must be in position to receive God's blessings. But we can't score the touchdowns in life until we have arrived at our position. Had Elisha not put in the time and work, he would never have been able to fill the role Elijah left.

Likewise, our Christian mentors expect us to read our Bible, improve our prayer life and strive to be more Christ-like every day. Only those willing to walk hand-in-hand with Christ will win in the end.

**It's time to get to work**

Elisha did receive the double portion of Elisha's blessing, and he became a well-respected prophet.

When Elijah went up to heaven Elisha's position in the kingdom shot up as well. Elisha took the cloak Elijah left him and struck the water of the Jordan, dividing it right and left. Then he crossed over. That symbolizes Elisha crossing over from being an understudy to a full-fledged prophet.

As a mentee, you will know when your lesson has been learned and it's time for you to assume your own set of responsibilities. You just have to make sure that you are ready to assume the position.

None of us can remain in our own worlds and not step out on faith to extend a helping hand to another believer. God may be calling you to be a mentor in the men's ministry or the women's ministry. You may be called take a young pastor under your arm or it may be simply reaching out to a friend and loved one and teaching them how to read and study the Bible.

Regardless of the task God assigns you, remember that you are being trusted to represent the Holy Spirit. Don't bother about the outcome of your spiritual relationship. Keep your eyes on the kingdom, and all else will be fine.

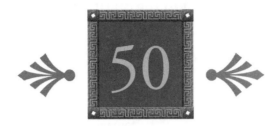

# Doing God's will should always be our first priority

*Text focus: Ephesians 6*
***

How many times have you ever prayed for something, only to be surprised and shocked that it didn't work out as you planned?

Take your pick: job, home, spouse and or children. No matter what it is, I'm sure many of us have at one time or another prayed to God that we blessed with something that we really, really wanted. Yet have you ever asked yourself, "Lord, is this your will for my life?"

Trust me, I've been there.

In my first marriage, I often thanked God for my wife. She had a wonderful smile, pleasing personality, was good looking and had a great job as a TV anchor. But it didn't take long for the marriage to sour, and after six years, it ended. What I discovered is that I spent a great deal of time thanking God for her, but never at one time did I ever ask, "God, is this the woman you set aside for me?"

I know some of you may very well be perplexed and find that what I'm saying is trivial or not really important. Some may even throw back the scripture that God will give you the desires of your heart. But that still doesn't mean it's what you need. It may very well be a want, but not a need.

This came to mind recently when I emailed Frank Turner, a Detroit TV news anchor, who was embroiled in a dispute with his station owners. It seems that Turner wanted to host his own radio show on a Christian radio station, but TV station officials said that conflicted with his contract with them. Turner took them to court, leading to a contentious battle with the station. He eventually decided to leave the TV station in order to do the radio show.

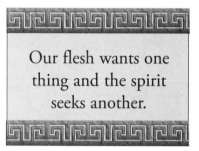

Our flesh wants one thing and the spirit seeks another.

I was curious as to what Turner's reasons were for trying to force the station's hand, so I sent him an email. He replied by asking why I was asking, and I told him that I wondered if God told him to take the course of action or if it was his choosing.

I really wanted Turner to respond, because it would have been great to find out if he was pushing the action, rather than have God lead him to the right decision.

There is no doubt that it was hard for Turner to give up a good six figure salary as a main TV anchor, but if it was God's will that was more important, He may have wanted Turner to leave one job to accept another. Some may have thought the TV job was better, but we never know God's reasons; the radio gig could have been what was needed — now.

I strongly believe that many people make the mistake of accepting jobs that on the surface look great, but in the long run, isn't good for their well being. Others may be in marriages that have gone wrong, unwilling to accept the position that maybe had they asked God if this is the person I should have married, they wouldn't be in that position. I've seen individuals mired in financial difficulty because they moved out of one house for a larger one, never wanting to admit that that wasn't the best decision.

My experience tells me that our flesh wants one thing and the spirit seeks another. We may very well have to go through the trials and tribulations before we wake up and realize one day that God simply wants us to come to Him and seek His guidance before we make such life changing positions.

Folks, there have been jobs that I would have loved to landed but the Lord said, "Roland, that's not for you." The pay was awesome, but God would never allow me to take the job. At one time, I wanted to return to my old job in Dallas running a newspaper, but God told me that under no circumstances could I accept the position unless three individuals were no longer employed there. Their mere presence polluted the place and God make it clear that I could not co-exist with them. I told the publisher that and he made a decision to keep them. That was fine. He did what was best for him, and I had to make a decision that was pleasing to God.

If you are having to make a decision in your life, take the time to step back and ask, "God, is this in your will?" You might be surprised at the answer you receive.

# ABOUT THE AUTHOR

Roland S. Martin is a nationally award-winning and multifaceted journalist.

A nationally syndicated columnist with Creators Syndicate, Mr. Martin is the author of *Listening to the Spirit Within: 50 Perspectives on Faith,* and *Speak, Brother! A Black Man's View of America.*

Mr. Martin is a commentator for TV One Cable Network also host of "The Roland S. Martin Show" on WVON-AM/1690 in Chicago. He can be heard daily from 6 a.m. to 9 a.m. He is also a CNN Contributor, appearing on a variety of shows, including Paula Zahn Now, Anderson Cooper 360, Lou Dobbs Tonight, and many others.

An insightful and provocative analyst, Mr. Martin has appeared numerous times on MSNBC, FOX News, Court TV, BET Nightly News, BBC News, National Public Radio, The Word Network, America's Black Forum, American Urban Radio Networks, the Tom Joyner Morning Show, and NPR's News and Notes.

Mr. Martin is a special correspondent for Essence Magazine, writing a bi-monthly column and blogging daily on Essence.com.

He is the former executive editor/general manager of the Chicago Defender, the nation's largest Black daily newspaper.

He is the former founding news editor for Savoy Magazine under the team of New York-based Vanguarde Media, and the former founding editor of BlackAmericaWeb.com, owned by nationally syndicated radio show host Tom Joyner and Radio One.

He previously served as owner/publisher of Dallas-Fort Worth Heritage, a Christian monthly newspaper. He also has worked as managing editor of the Houston Defender and the Dallas Weekly, which he led to a number of local, state and national journalism awards. Mr. Martin has worked as morning drive reporter for KRLD/1080 AM; news director and morning anchor at KKDA-AM in Dallas; city hall reporter for the Fort Worth Star-Telegram; and county government and neighbors reporter for the Austin American-Statesman.

He has won more than 20 professional awards for journalistic excellence, including a regional Edward R. Murrow Award from the Radio Television News

Directors; several first place awards from the Dallas-Fort Worth Association of Black Communicators; two citations from the National Associated Press-Managing Editors Conference; the top sports reporting award in 1997 from the National Association of Black Journalists; and honors from the Houston Press Club.

Mr. Martin is a member of the National Association of Black Journalists, Alpha Phi Alpha Fraternity, Inc., and the American Society of Newspaper Editors.

He is a 1987 graduate of Jack Yates High School-Magnet School of Communications, and a 1991 graduate of Texas A&M University, where he earned a bachelor's of science degree in journalism. Martin is studying to receive his master's degree in Christian Communications at Louisiana Baptist University.

He is married to the Rev. Jacquie Hood Martin, author of Fulfilled! The Art and Joy of Balanced Living. They reside in Chicago and Dallas.

ROMAR Media Group Release
www.rolandsmartin.com

# Speak, Brother!
## *A Black Man's View of America*
Roland S. Martin

Unrelenting, uncompromising and downright honest Roland S. Martin offers a bold and fresh perspective for the 21st century. Martin has covered a variety of stories and newsmakers in his 14 years as a professional journalist. An in the course of doing so he has gained a significant insight into the triumphs and failings of this country's best and brightest. He tackles a variety of issues with passion, knowledge and spirituality. Whether it's commentaries on sports, social justice, business or the media, Roland S. Martin refuses to be pigeonholed as a conservative or a liberal, Democrat or a Republican. As he puts it, he is simply "a Black man in America."

"This is Martin at his in-your-face best. Whether he's roasting the mainstream media for its lack of diversity, Puff Daddy and Destiny's Child for their spiritual hypocrisy, or Charles Barkley for his portrait in chains, Martin is right on, a voice that cannot be ignored."

Tim Madigan, author, The Burning: Massacre, Destruction and the Tulsa Race Riot of *1921*

"Roland Martin is a voice of reason, rage and unwavering blackness. He is a 21st century 'race man,' cut from the same mold that produced the angry voices of the 1920s Harlem Renaissance and the 1960s Black Power Movement."

*DeWayne Wickham, columnist, USA Today and Gannett News Service*

0-9719107-2-3 $9.95